Praise for

The Secret Solution

"*The Secret Solution* is a great read that perfectly blends *What Great Principals Do Differently* and an enjoyable fiction novel. This book is a must-read for any aspiring new or veteran principals. As you follow Roger Rookie on his journey as a principal, you'll likely recognize several common issues encountered in any school and learn from how he overcomes these obstacles to transform his school. Enjoy an easy read while learning how to improve your school with *The Secret Solution!*"

—Jessica Johnson, principal/district assessment coordinator, Dodgeland Elementary School, Dodgeland, Wisconsin, coauthor of *The Coach Approach to School Leadership* and *Breaking Out of Isolation*

"*The Secret Solution* is an easy read and a powerful guide to help leaders know as much of what *not* to do, as well as a practical formula for success. This book is a great example of how to cultivate greatness within yourself in order to be able to mentor the others around you to their potential. Anyone who is venturing down a path of campus management will benefit from the mistakes and lessons learned from *The Secret Solution*."

—Amber Teamann, principal, Whitt Elementary, Wylie, Texas

"Whitaker, Miller, and Donlan hit a home run with *The Secret Solution*. Not only does the book paint a vivid picture of the complexities of leading school change for aspiring school leaders but it also provides reflective dialogue for experienced educational administrators. The parables within depict mistakes and lessons learned in a quick and easy, weekend reading format."

—Matt Townsley, director of instruction, Solon Community Schools, Solon, Iowa

"If you've ever constructed a jigsaw puzzle, you know that in order to create the entire picture, you need to find the border pieces, build the large images that appear in the photo on the outer box, and navigate the pieces that comprise the subtle background colors. Like a jigsaw puzzle, school leadership comprises many different pieces—all intricate in their own ways, but also all necessary to create the big picture. *The Secret Solution: How One Principal Discovered the Path to Success* by Todd Whitaker, Sam Miller, and Ryan Donlan is an easy-to-read parable about a principal's journey through the nuances of school leadership. Through descriptions of different leadership styles—as well as many of the steps and missteps that building administrators often take in an effort to create change, build climate, and cultivate school culture—the book celebrates the value of mentors, collegiality, and human relationships. With its amusing dialogue and thought-provoking graphics, *The Secret Solution* is a must-have for anyone entering into or new to the principalship. For veteran administrators, this book offers a valuable reflection on roads traveled, pitfalls to avoid, and practices to cultivate for continued success."

—**Mike Pinto**, principal, James Cole Elementary School, Lafayette, Indiana

THE SECRET SOLUTION

How one Principal Discovered the Path to Success

Todd Whitaker, Sam Miller, and Ryan Donlan

Illustrations by
Eric Cleveland and Ryan Donlan

The Secret Solution

This book is available at special discounts when purchased in quantity for use as premiums, promotions, fundraisers, or for educational use. For inquiries and details, contact the publisher at books@daveburgessconsulting.com.

Published by Dave Burgess Consulting, Inc.
San Diego, CA
http://daveburgessconsulting.com

Cover Design by Genesis Kohler
Editing and Interior Design by My Writers' Connection

Library of Congress Control Number: 2017961372
Paperback ISBN: 978-1-946444-48-6
Ebook ISBN: 978-1-946444-49-3

First Printing: April 2018

Contents

Chapter 1
The Big Night 1

Chapter 2
Roger Rookie's First Makeover: The Hibernator.....19

Chapter 3
Roger Rookie's Next Makeover: The Glad-Hander...37

Chapter 4
Roger Rookie's Third Makeover: The Thumb........71

Chapter 5
Roger Rookie's Final Makeover: The Pathfinder....101

Chapter 6
 Back to the Big Night . . . "That's a Wrap"...........123

The Epilogue..127

More From Dave Burgess Consulting............137

About the Authors..149

Cast of Characters
of Anywhere Middle School
(In Order of Their Appearance, in a Town Near *You*)

Roger Rookie – New principal of Anywhere Middle School

Carol Charming – Eager, young local newspaper reporter

Ned Neverthere – Former principal who was a bit out of touch

Nellie Newcomer – New, enthusiastic teacher, ready to make a difference

Mildred Morose – Negative veteran staff member who thrives on "a following"

Judy Slacker – Veteran teacher who will go the extra mile—for the extra pay

Karl Chameleon – Eighth-year math teacher who goes with the flow

LaVon Babble – If it isn't good enough, it wouldn't be the minimum

Trudy Savage – Office secretary and executioner (Just try to take a box of paper clips without asking. Just try!)

Kris Bliss – The personable, friendly front-office receptionist

Sandy Starr – The most respected and effective teacher in the school

Edgar Sleeper – Social studies teacher, losing his luster (he hangs with a toxic crowd)

Joel Gerrymander – Roger's friend, principal/athletic director from a neighboring school—schmoozer, manipulator, and high-speed multi-tasker ("Fire, Ready, Aim!")

Cindy Sage – Superintendent's secretary of thirty years: dignified, maternal, and wise

Ivan Ironside – Ex-military captain and neighboring town's current middle school principal (Don't mess around with this guy.)

Chapter 1
The Big Night

It was Roger Rookie's big night.

He couldn't believe it! In a few minutes, he would be recognized as this year's "Super Apple" award winner by the State Principals Association. *Be sure to thank all the teachers in your acceptance speech*, he reminded himself. They had worked so hard and had come so far. Winning this award had taken a team effort. Boy, was he proud!

As Roger sat in the small room adjacent the ceremony, the door opened, and in walked Carol Charming from the big newspaper in town.

Wow! The local reporter is here to ask ME some questions! Roger beamed.

Roger stood as Carol reached out to shake his hand. "I'm pleased to meet you, Mr. Rookie."

"As am I, Ms. Charming, and please call me Roger."

"Only if I'm Carol."

"You got it, Carol."

"Well, Roger, you have a big night ahead of you. Do you have a few minutes to talk?"

"Certainly. I don't think I'm on for about another fifteen or twenty minutes," he said and gestured for her to have a seat in one of the chairs. *She seems very nice*, he thought to himself. *I hope I make a favorable impression.*

"I'd like to start, Roger, by saying 'Congratulations.' You must be so proud. You're receiving one of the highest honors in the entire state. I bet everyone at Anywhere Middle School feels lucky to have you as principal. Your job must come so easy for you. What is your secret?!"

Roger half smiled and paused before responding, "I have asked myself that same question probably a hundred times, Carol. If you had seen me in

1

my first year, you would never have used the word 'easy'! I wasn't sure I was going to make it through my first week!"

"No way," she said.

"Yes, way!" Roger chuckled. "I've got to be honest. At first, I wasn't even sure who I really was as a leader. In those early days, survival was my only ambition. Trust me, no one would have guessed I would ever be on stage accepting an award for doing something positive. I didn't have a clue. I tried on different styles of leadership, all the while searching for the path to success. Searching for *the secret*."

Carol seemed startled by his response. "I would have never guessed you struggled starting out. How did you go from that sort of start to being today's award winner? Especially in just two years! I'd love to hear more!"

Roger laughed. "To say I struggled would be a huge understatement. I figured the only award I might get was the 'Shortest Stint as Principal.' Let me tell you a story about how I started and how far I've come."

"That would be great!" said Carol. "Education's my favorite beat. I love to report great news on schools, especially the 'come from behind' stories!"

Roger Rookie thought back to the beginning of his journey just two years prior. He remembered his first day as principal of Anywhere Middle School . . .

A Call from the Boss

Ring . . . ringgg . . . ringgggggg.

"Hello, Roger Rookie here."

"Rookie, as soon as you're done unpacking, I want to see you in my office," said Mr. Superintendent.

"Yes sir, I'll be right over."

Roger dropped everything and hurried over to Mr. Superintendent's office.

As he drove the few short blocks to the central office, he thought, *Gosh! I wonder what he wants. It's pretty early for a trip to the boss's office.*

The Big Night

The door was open, and Mr. Superintendent waved him in and pointed to a chair across from his desk. "Rookie," Mr. Superintendent began, "You're an impressive kid with what I believe to be a lot of potential, but I don't have a lot of time for your care and feeding. I have board members all over me who want results."

"Results, sir?" Rogers said, shifting in his chair.

"Yeah, results! Learning results!"

"What I need you to do *immediately* is to turn Anywhere Middle School around, plain and simple. I want every adult in your school who works with students to value the learning that goes on, not just the teaching. And at this point, Rookie, I don't even think your team values its teaching as much as it does its teachers! We're not here to create salaries for adults, young man; we're here for the learning of children! I want results, not just 'forming a committee for *this*' or 'meeting with stakeholders for *that*.' I want that place turned around.

"And, Rookie, I want accountability. No time to cry about the labor pains; just show me the baby! Test results are in the tank. Every *single* time that Lois Lane upstart from our local newspaper writes another story, it seems the school down the road looks better than ours. I think her name's Charming . . . Carol Charming."

"Should I develop a relationship with her, sir?" Roger asked.

"I don't care what you do in your spare time, Rookie, just keep it out of the headlines."

"I meant . . . "

"Rookie, they say Charming has a nose for news. Well, I'll tell you, she has a nose all right, because she's always sniffin' around for something. Usually it's for evidence of student learning, test scores in particular. Darn it, when our standardized test scores post the next time around, I want them smelling like roses!"

"They will, sir!" Roger assured him.

"That's what I want to hear, kid, cause I'm tired of looking like a fool. Not gonna happen anymore!"

"No, it won't, sir."

"You got smart people working there. I know; I hired most of them. Some I even taught with, back in the day. Something's wrong, though. I'm not sure what it is, but the students and their parents—and even the teachers—don't seem to value learning like people did when I taught there."

"I'll figure it out, sir."

"Darn tootin' you will, Rookie! Find out what's wrong, and fix it. Don't spend a lot of money either! When Neverthere was principal, every time I asked him a question, it seemed he didn't even know what was going on in those classrooms. Can't figure out why! Seemed to have a good head on his shoulders, that Neverthere. But he was clueless!"

"I'll try to have a clue, sir."

"You bet you will, Rookie! Son, you got your marching orders. Any questions?"

"No sir. I'll get that school whipped into shape in no time. I'll figure out the secret! I'll find that path toward a focus on learning. I'll find us a path to success! You can count on Roger Rookie."

Shiny New Office

The sign on the door at Anywhere Middle School (AMS) read: *Mr. Roger Rookie, Principal.* Being a brand-new principal, Roger smiled every time he saw his name on the door. Sometimes he even said it to himself, "Principal Rookie." It had a nice ring to it.

When no one was looking, Roger used the cuff of his shirt to polish the nameplate so it looked nice and shiny. Looking at his reflection, Roger would point and say, "You da man!"

This was his first job as a school administrator. He was stoked.

Roger had always known he wanted to be an educator. He started college with a clear focus as a future teacher, a future *difference maker*. College only deepened his excitement. He loved his classes—at least most of them. He learned a lot (from most professors, anyway) and was so excited when he finally had the chance to practice teaching his senior year.

I was the best darn thing to happen to education in quite some time, he mused. *You 'da man!*

Plus, he was geeked the first time someone called him "Mr. Rookie" and even remembered thinking at the time, *I can put that on my business cards. Well, if teachers had business cards.*

The teacher who supervised Roger during his student/teaching internship, Mr. Indifferent, was closing in on retirement. He saw Roger as "free labor" and allowed Roger to entirely take over the classroom on his second day!

Of course, he'd had a few missteps, but "Mr. Rookie" gradually won over the students and developed a balance of building relationships and setting high expectations. He was a go-getter and started applying for teaching jobs early in his final semester.

Through good fortune and hard work, I'll have my first teaching position before graduation day! Roger promised himself.

And he did.

Roger Rookie loved teaching, and he soon learned he could make an even bigger impact on his students by continuing his education. He started a master's degree program in school administration because it looked like fun. Plus all the older teachers at his school (no administrators—they were just in it for the pay increase) told stories about weekend classes, some of which were held at hotels in destination cities. Food, drinks, not too much homework. Yep, those classes were the best!

While taking those classes, he remembered entertaining his first thoughts about someday becoming a principal. *A principalship might be something I'll do if I get tired of teaching. It seems as if the principals I have known have all been a little tired of something.*

It turned out the timing for his master's program was perfect. Just as Roger earned his degree, the district adjacent to where he taught announced its principal's plan to retire. Friends joked with him that he should put the tuition money he'd invested to good use and throw his hat into the race. Roger knew he wouldn't get past the first round because that particular district always hired from within. Even the superintendent used to teach at one the district's schools.

Peer pressure and a bit of friendly banter from his friend, Joel Gerrymander, an athletic director/assistant principal in a neighboring town, led him to say, "I might as well give it a crack. Plus the big office would be a nice bonus!"

So he applied. And then took a lot of ribbing from his friends for being so bold. Even his mom thought it was "cute" that he thought he had a chance. He was soooo young!

But a few interviews later, and "Mr. Roger Rookie" was announced as the new principal of Anywhere Middle School! Roger was both elated and terrified. *Oh, my goodness!* he thought after accepting the position. *What did I get myself into? Being responsible for an entire school is a BIG DEAL. I'd better do my homework. I WILL be ready for this.*

Roger continued to feel that mix of nerves and excitement as he set up his shiny new office. The anticipation brewed right up until he got the call from Mr. Superintendent. Now he had a whole new list of concerns.

With so many thoughts and ideas racing through his head, Roger decided he needed to get things prioritized. He scratched down an "I'm a Principal Now" to-do list on the new notepad he bought at the college bookstore. He was always writing notes to himself and drawing pictures. Doing so kept him from having to remember everything in his head. Plus he liked to doodle.

Let's see. . . a focus on learning, he pondered.

As he sketched, Roger imagined the first day of school, staff arriving ready to follow his lead on a path toward better learning. Students would step up for the young, hip principal. Staff too! And, after all, he had a master's degree. *How hard could this be?*

Roger did his best thinking late at night. With bag of popcorn in hand, soft drink at the ready, and his favorite late-night TV shows playing, he thought about what his new role would entail.

"I'm a principal now" to-do LIST...

1.
2.
3.
4.
5.

Lea rning

what would a
FOCUS ON LEARNING
LOOK LIKE?

I chose education to make a difference. This new gig is a way to have an even broader influence. Heck, I don't know much about Anywhere Middle School, but if you have seen one school, you've seen them all, haven't you? I'll discover the secret to this leadership thing in no time. I'll whip that school into shape!

But Roger had not heard very good things about Anywhere Middle School, or Mr. Neverthere, the previous principal, for that matter. He rubbed his hands together, wrote down a few more thoughts and ideas on his notepad, and anxiously thought of the teachers and students who were to report that fall.

Let's See Focus on Learning
QUICK!

What's the secret? The Path??
"here's thoughts"

- Start upbeat, with confidence
- Give a PEP talk!
- But my textbook says,

"First watch, wait to Act"
   and "Don't rock the boat"
and "Avoid the potholes."

Hmmm
- Fake it 'til you make it, right?!?

OK, I'm ready.
LET'S DO IT!

First Faculty Meeting

As Roger reviewed his notes, he was both excited and nervous. It was his first faculty meeting, it was the teachers' first day back from summer break, and he was "on duty" to meet his staff and fire up his troops! His last thought as he walked into the room for the meeting was, *I am going to change Anywhere Middle School.*

Looking at the group of teachers before him, Roger introduced himself and shared a little about his background. He closed with, "I know you're all very excited to move this school forward!" and expected thunderous applause, or at least a smattering of claps. When no one budged, he added, "So don't hesitate to show me what you've got!! We're going to reinvent this school's reputation!"

What Roger got instead was a rousing round of "look."

Fumbling a bit, he introduced Nellie Newcomer, the newest addition to the AMS faculty, and asked her to share a little bit about herself.

"Hi, I'm Nellie Newcomer, recent graduate from How-to-Be-a-Teacher College. I'm very excited to begin decorating my classroom and getting to know all of you. I hope to quickly learn about how things work around here so I can get more involved and make a difference. It will be nice meeting you all."

Nellie seemed a little nervous when she talked but got through it okay. She did get embarrassed when someone in the back muttered, "They hired *her* over my nephew? I wonder whom she's related to."

Roger chose to ignore the comment, proceeded through several management tasks, and read some rules from the handbook. He then shifted to school reform, as he had just read something about it in his last college class.

"A principal's job is to be an 'instructional leader,' and thus I plan on visiting classrooms every day. I'm going to learn from the great work you're doing! Together we are going to focus on learning and put Anywhere Middle School's name in lights!"

He then shared that AMS needed to do something about its test scores.

"Central office had a meeting last week and said everyone needs to increase the performance on the state exams, so we need to really make this a focus this year."

The Big Night

As Roger stood in front of the group with a big smile on his face, one teacher, Mildred Morose, stood. She placed hand on hip and held a bent finger in the air. She then looked over her eyeglasses at Roger and said loudly, "Excuse me, but I didn't know we had a problem at Anywhere Middle School. I've been here over thirty years, and I think this is a pretty good school. And if we want to improve anything here, maybe somebody should do something about these students. I don't know how we can raise test scores with kids and parents who don't care. If it doesn't matter to them, then I don't see why it should matter to us. You can lead a horse to water, as they say. . ."

Roger looked around the room. Several teachers nodded in agreement with Mildred Morose. He even thought he heard someone whisper, "Amen, sister!" He felt his face flush in embarrassment, but he gathered his thoughts and said, "What I mean to say is we will build on the great work that is already being done at AMS."

A couple of people in the back of the room snickered but did not comment.

After a short pause, Roger continued to go through the items on his agenda. He noticed that, as he was discussing attendance procedures, a handful of teachers were talking with each other somewhat loudly. He also saw a teacher knitting and two doing crossword puzzles or sudoku puzzles. Roger ignored the distractions but felt very uncomfortable. By the end of the faculty meeting, Roger could not avoid the fact that only a handful of teachers still appeared to be listening to what he was saying.

Feeling awkward, Roger quickly ended the meeting.

Back in his office, Roger was working at his desk when he looked up and saw a teacher standing in his doorway.

"Hello, Mr. Rookie. I'm Ms. Slacker, and I would like to thank you, first of all, for such a short faculty meeting. The teachers at AMS have so much to do in preparing for our students; it's good to have a leader who understands this."

Roger appreciated the compliment but felt a bit uneasy accepting it, as the short meeting was not his intent.

Judy Slacker went on. "As you have mentioned your role as our instructional leader, you must understand that young Nellie Newcomer needs a mentor. Always one willing to serve in the best interests of children and, of course, with commensurate compensation, I am volunteering my twenty-seven years of experience to be Miss Newcomer's mentor."

Roger readied what was to be a taken-under-advisement response, but Judy continued. "I have already spoken with the other teachers in the department, and they all agreed it was only fair for me to get the extra stipend to mentor Nellie. I have the most seniority; however, with all the new changes that have been thrown at us teachers in the past few years, I think the pitiful stipend to serve as a mentor should be increased. I would be happy to work with you on an appropriate stipend for my hard work to help Miss Newcomer become a great teacher like me."

Roger, smiling on the outside, tried to envision a diplomatic solution that would result in Judy's not mentoring Miss Newcomer. His mind raced. With the first impression Judy Slacker gave Roger, and especially with the quick comment about the compensation involved, it did not take a rocket scientist to conclude Judy did not appear to be "student centered."

Nellie Newcomer's excellent interview and reference checks indicated she was going to be a fantastic teacher, focused 100 percent on the children. Nellie was Roger's first hire, so he felt particularly responsible ensuring she got the support she was going to need in her first year.

"Ms. Slacker, I just don't quite know where I want to go with this," Roger said, searching for a way out, and seeing none. "However, since you have made it a point to talk with others, and because we probably should begin providing some assistance to Nellie right away, why don't we give it a go?"

"Good decision, Mr. Rookie. It is what we as a faculty would expect."

Roger turned and said, "When do you think you and Nellie might. . . "

Judy Slacker was already out the office door, en route to the teachers' lounge, passing Nellie Newcomer along the way without a word.

Not a bad idea: a quick lounge visit, Roger thought. *I need to be in touch with my faculty.* He walked into the teachers' lounge to get a cup of coffee and noticed quite a few teachers looked surprised to see the principal in the *teachers'* lounge.

Roger poured a cup of coffee and sat down next to Karl Chameleon. Karl was in his eighth year of teaching mathematics. Roger asked Karl how his summer break had been. Karl quickly launched into a very long story about his vacation with his family to Mount Rushmore.

Nice enough guy, Roger thought. *Family man.*

He was getting ready to make a comment about Karl's adventure when another teacher, LaVon Babble, asked Roger, "Mr. Rookie, given that my daycare provider cannot watch my children after school, would you have a problem if I left school early on Mondays, Wednesdays, and Fridays?"

Others listened with interest.

LaVon continued, "I can leave at the end of the last period when students are leaving, but know that on those days, I'll come in early to make up the time. This is really the same arrangement I had with Mr. Neverthere. I wanted to ask you, as a courtesy, but I'm sure you will support your faculty with things such as this."

She concluded by noting the arrangement had worked out well in the past, calling it a "win/win."

Other teachers chimed in quickly, sharing that teachers work many evenings and weekends, and leaving a little early on occasion was not a big deal.

Roger mumbled, "Let me give this some thought, Mrs. Babble," then got up and walked out of the room.

Later, at the end of the day, Roger looked up from his desk and noticed Nellie Newcomer was standing at the door.

She smiled and said, "I want to thank you again, Mr. Rookie, for giving me an opportunity as a teacher. I'm not going to let you down."

Roger responded, "Thank you, Nellie; that's nice to hear. Please, if you need any help, do not hesitate to ask." He continued, "You will be interested to know I have assigned Ms. Slacker as your mentor."

Her face dimmed.

"I'm hoping Judy will provide you with the support you are going to need as a first-year teacher." Roger questioned whether he believed this statement himself but tried not to let his doubts show.

Parent Meeting

On the second day of AMS's back-to-school workshop, Roger had a meeting scheduled with the Johnson family. They had two students attending AMS. It didn't take long in the meeting to learn that the family was upset with the school secretary.

Anywhere Middle School had two secretaries in the main office. The primary secretary was Trudy Savage. Beyond the imposing, deeply riveted symmetry of her furrowed brow, Trudy Savage's entire visage resembled that of a praying mantis, poised to pounce and paralyze victims with a barb of her sharp tongue and quickly devour their exposed necks, leaving their lifeless corpses for grazing (and, of course, deterrence for those who might dare cross her path).

Trudy Savage was well known throughout the community for her lack of people skills and overall negative attitude. She wasn't too fond of students—or adults, for that matter. Her comments to parents, students, and staff were often shockingly rude: "Last time I looked in the mirror, I was the one running this office," was one of her favorite phrases along with, "There's something to be said for apples and trees, don't you think?"

Parents routinely reported being treated poorly by Mrs. Savage. It was no surprise that everyone tried to avoid her whenever possible.

The other secretary, Kris Bliss, was friendly and helpful—and the "most busy."

Teachers and parents quickly learned that Kris was the secretary with whom to have all conversations in the office. She was the one who helped folks and considered everyone at Anywhere Middle School her extended family. Kris had pictures of her family adorning her office area, along with scented candles and thank you notes of appreciation.

The only decoration on Trudy Savage's desk was a calendar that read: "Take a number. Better yet, *deal with it yourself!*"

As Roger met with the Johnson family in his office, Mrs. Johnson explained they were there because Trudy Savage had told her, "If you can't afford the registration fees, you need to think about getting a job to support your children properly. You don't want this cycle to repeat itself, do you?"

Roger was stunned. He knew Mrs. Savage lacked interpersonal skills, but this comment was way out of bounds.

I wonder if I should ask Mrs. Savage to join us in the meeting to present her side of the story, Roger pondered. *Probably not. Her presence would only make things worse.*

He explained, "I'm so very sorry you were treated this way. It does not represent how we should be partnering with our families at Anywhere Middle School. Please know I will definitely investigate your concerns."

The Johnsons thanked Roger Rookie for meeting with them and listening to their issues.

Roger never met with Trudy Savage about the Johnsons' complaint; rather, he chose to avoid the problem.

He didn't want his head devoured.

Reading Department Meeting

The reading department was excited to meet with Roger Rookie. The department consisted of seven teachers, and, unlike some of the other AMS departments, they worked well together.

Sandy Starr, department head, had been trying to arrange a meeting with her department and Roger Rookie since his first day on the job, but he kept postponing the meeting, as he quickly learned he had much on his plate. The urgencies of each day seemed to take priority. It was now a month into the school year. Mrs. Starr finally had pinned him down.

Sandy Starr had a reputation for being an outstanding teacher. Roger had reviewed her student achievement data and noted that it was significantly higher than almost all other teachers at AMS. Mrs. Starr opened the meeting with introductions and announcements.

For Roger's benefit, she said, "Our department had been working for over a year on how to improve the reading skills of students who were multiple years below grade level. Unlike the elementary, AMS did not have a program designed specifically for its struggling readers. That changed when we learned about a research-based reading program designed for secondary students." She reported that several schools had implemented the program and had seen significant increases in student achievement data. "We, as reading teachers, are excited and feel like we have finally discovered a reading program that is perfect for AMS. We would like to share some of the details with you, Mr. Rookie, on why we feel this way."

As the teachers took turns describing the specifics of the program, Roger Rookie quietly listened. He asked a few clarifying questions but did not appear too interested in learning about the program. In truth, he was having a hard time focusing on the reading program because his thoughts kept drifting back to Trudy Savage, the Johnson's, and the debacle of his first staff meeting.

Finally, after the department finished its presentation, Sandy Starr asked, "Mr. Rookie, what are your thoughts on implementing the program at AMS?"

"It brings with it a number of factors to consider and is worthy of a closer look," said Roger, thanking the reading department for their hard work and noting he would consider their request.

Hmmm, that's a positive step. Those folks seem to be focused on learning, he thought as he walked back to his office. *Maybe the secret to better learning at Anywhere Middle School is just looking, listening, not rocking the boat, and letting faculty come up with better plans for instruction.*

Roger agreed that the reading program sounded good; at least the parts he caught during the presentation sounded good. But he didn't know if Central Office would respond favorably to the idea. He got a sense the district leaders were not interested in doing things that would increase spending. *I'm not sure I want to go down that road with my superintendent right now,* he thought. *Although our scores in reading really do need to improve, I'm not sure I can spend any money. Better hold off. Better not make waves.*

Chapter 2
Roger Rookie's First Makeover: The Hibernator

A week later, Roger was in the hallway just around the corner from the main office when he heard Trudy Savage yell, "Come to me 'My Pretty.' I've been waiting to see you!" Worried about what Trudy was up to, he watched and listened from an angle, just out of her line of sight.

He cringed as Trudy launched into Nellie Newcomer for "pilfering" extra markers from the storeroom. Roger saw Nellie's face redden. She was clearly horrified. Obviously, no one had warned her about following the "Trudy rules." Taking supplies without her approval was the number one unwritten rule a teacher did not break.

"Do you mean to tell me, *young thing*, given the fact that you purportedly received an education prior to your arrival, they didn't teach you in 'being-a-teacher school' to get permission before taking things that aren't yours? We teach *that* to children in kindergarten!!"

Before Nellie had a chance to apologize, Trudy Savage began pointing her finger, yelling that taking supplies without proper authorization was unprofessional and that Mr. Rookie would be notified promptly.

Nellie almost started crying.

A parent in the office quietly walked out.

A couple of boys who had been sent to the office paced outside, afraid to go in—and equally afraid of Mrs. Savage's wrath if they didn't enter to *Sit in Shame*, as she required.

Roger did not know what to do, so he quietly walked through the office door, pretending to be unaware of what had just transpired. He moved into his office, closing the door and sitting down at his desk.

He hesitated and thought to himself, *Well, Trudy IS Trudy. It's probably best to let her "regulate." She's keeping more work off my desk by setting the tone. And*

I need to spend my time finding the secret to this learning thing. She's probably one to "Never Smile till November." Though I do hope November comes quickly!

Nellie Newcomer left the office upset. Roger rubbed his neck uncomfortably and opened his email, thinking of something a principal would send to his staff to help increase the focus on learning.

Nellie needed some support, so she went to visit her designated mentor, Judy Slacker. She was just about to enter Judy's classroom when she heard her talking with Mildred Morose.

"You know, Mildred, the one thing I always say about the start of a new school year: It's a great feeling. . . until those darned kids arrive."

"Tell me about it! I don't know if it's too much television or family trees without branches, but something's sure wrong with these children nowadays!" Mildred added.

They both cackled.

Gathering her nerve, Nellie walked in, and the teachers continued ranting about students and even some of the other adults in the building. Nellie couldn't believe what they were saying—how rude and downright mean they were being. After several more minutes of the gossip session, Judy Slacker turned to Nellie Newcomer with a *what do you want?* glare.

"Well, don't just stand there, Miss Newcomer. What is so important it can't possibly wait until the next lunch period in the lounge to discuss?" Ms. Slacker asked.

"Mrs. Savage just yelled at me in the office for taking supplies. She did this in front of everyone, and I feel as low as a carpet fiber. I hope I'm not in trouble with Mr. Rookie," she said. "Mrs. Savage threatened to turn me in to him."

Judy Slacker and Mildred Morose laughed.

"Oh, come *on*, dearie," said Mildred. "Everyone knows you don't just take things from Trudy Savage's office. You're lucky she didn't chop off your hand at the knuckle or chew on your neck."

"Haven't you learned the 'Anywhere Way' yet, little lady?" Judy added. "C'mon newbie; toughen up. You're in big-girl school now."

As they continued to laugh, Nellie Newcomer left the classroom and walked back to her room feeling embarrassed and lonely.

The Bullies

Roger Rookie discovered in his first few weeks that the Anywhere Middle School staff had a pecking order. He privately referred to the dominant group of teachers as the Bullies. He had actually been warned about them prior to taking his post as principal. The Bullies had a few main members: Mildred Morose, Judy Slacker, and LaVon Babble. Edgar Sleeper seemed to hang with them quite a bit but didn't say much. He was sort of like their lap dog.

Mildred Morose was the ringleader. She was one of the most veteran teachers in the district and was not afraid to engage in conflict with anybody, including the principal—something Roger had discovered the hard way during his fateful first faculty meeting. She was loud, domineering, and confrontational. A select group of students were loyal to her, almost cult-like; they were her minions and treated others as outcasts. In short, they were learning from her how to treat others—and how to get exactly what they wanted. What was disappointing to Roger was the fact the staff did not seem upset by Mildred's behavior. He could not understand why they tolerated her dominance and didn't stand up to her.

Judy Slacker was also a veteran teacher and was almost as bad as Mildred. Her constant negative comments and condescending nature made her the last teacher he would ever want his own child to have. Unlike in Mildred's case, no students worshiped Judy, but they didn't seem to mind being in her class either. It was routine and didn't require much of them: day after day they read the text, did worksheets, turned things in, and repeated the process while Ms. Slacker sat at her computer. Kids could be invisible in Ms. Slacker's class.

LaVon Babble had been at AMS about ten years. She was not as bad as Mildred or Judy, but she was always at their side. She mostly did personal business during school hours: online shopping, telephone calls, and even paying her bills while kids read and did worksheets. She stood with the Bullies in the hallway between classes, urging students to get to class—even though she was in no hurry to get to her own.

Trading insider jokes was more the rule than the exception with the Bullies. They always ate together at the same lounge table and carried a small list of student mishaps to share with others at the students' expense. They had unflattering nicknames for everyone, even each other.

Despite some of the major problems at AMS, the Bullies appeared to like how the school was operating. At least, they liked how it was running for *them*. Others vied for their affection. Rumor had it that one time a few years back, Edgar Sleeper was sitting in the lounge with his feet up on the table when Mr. Neverthere stopped by his classroom for a formal classroom evaluation. When he didn't find Edgar in his class—although his students were there playing cards—Mr. Neverthere stormed down the hall until he found Edgar in the lounge. Mr. Neverthere stated, "Edgar, I was just in your classroom!"

Edgar responded, "Well, boss . . . is everything goin' ok?"

The Bullies had big fun with that one.

Edgar Sleeper was awarded their merit badge that day.

Karl Chameleon now tried for it every so often. The role of bully didn't fit him quite so well, but he was trying it on for size more frequently. Deep down, Roger was actually a bit afraid of Mildred Morose. He hated the fact that he allowed her to have power, but the truth was she was scary.

Turning to his in-box, Roger had a big smile on his face as he reread the congratulatory email from central office:

Dear Principal Rookie: On behalf of the superintendent and central office leadership team, we would like to commend you for getting your attendance reports turned in before any other principal in the district. Your proactivity in meeting our deadlines helps further the cause for school improvement and district-wide accountability.

In little time, Roger had established a reputation with central office for responding to its requests very quickly. Roger took great pride in making sure his business was conducted efficiently and on time. This required him to spend a lot of time in his office, sometimes with the door closed.

Roger took out his notebook and jotted down a few things he felt were keeping him on track.

STAYIN' ON TRACK

- Any good business must run like a machine.
- Keeping the gears running smoothly is key.
- Avoiding bumps in production is Principal's job.
- That'll probably HELP LEARNING.
- No side roads, no detours
- Gotta keep the train on the tracks ▦▦▦▦▦→
- No time to lay down new tracks.
- Keep the Train A-Movin'.
- That's probably the SECRET!

Meanwhile, beyond the closed doors of his office . . .

Teachers' Lounge

Nellie Newcomer grabbed her sack lunch and headed to the teachers' lounge. As she walked in, she heard Mildred Morose ask, "Has anybody seen our fearless principal in the last two weeks? It must be nice to earn a fat check and sit in your office all day playing solitaire. Trudy Savage told me she makes most of the decisions and does it for one-third the pay."

Laughter bubbled around the room.

Nellie felt uncomfortable.

Karl Chameleon mentioned, "Hey folks, I have a friend who teaches at Central Middle School. Last week they scheduled a staff meeting at someone's house for a fall get-together. Guess they even had a barbecue! Wonder why 'Rookie' never schedules any fun activities for our staff? We do a lot of great things here, and nobody ever recognizes what we do."

Judy Slacker took her turn to lambaste Roger Rookie. "You're not going to believe that over two weeks ago, I asked for a parking spot next to the building because I was having problems with my foot, as you all know of that planter's wart bunion fiasco I've been dealing with along with that rash. Anyway, 'Rookie' told me he would have to get back to me. Didn't happen! Hasn't happened! I think the reason our boy toy hides in his office all day is so he doesn't have to face me. If I don't get an answer soon, I'm going to sick Mildred on him. I don't think he wants any part of her."

Mildred Morose offered a sinister grin that made everyone in the lounge laugh—everyone except Nellie.

Nellie Newcomer did not think the others' comments were funny; in fact, they were completely disrespectful. But even she had misgivings about Roger Rookie's leadership. When Roger Rookie hired her, he told her he would be in her classroom to provide her with support. He had not been in her classroom since the first week of school, however. That was for only a minute to tell her about some paperwork that needed to be turned in.

Nellie hated the way she felt in the teachers' lounge. As she looked around, it dawned on her who was in the teachers' lounge: Mildred Morose, Judy Slacker, Karl Chameleon, Edgar Sleeper, LaVon Babble, and a handful of others. Nellie also noticed who wasn't in the lounge—whom she *never* saw in the teachers' lounge: teachers she actually enjoyed being around, teachers like Sandy Starr. Nellie decided this would be her last trip to the teachers' lounge and that she needed to pay Sandy Starr a visit.

What Superstars Do

Sandy Starr was putting student work on a wall when Nellie Newcomer knocked on her door.

"Come in, please. It's so nice to see you, Nellie," Sandy said with a smile.

Sandy offered Nellie her "teacher's" chair while she pulled up a student chair.

Sandy apologized to Nellie for not stopping by her room in the past couple of weeks. She had made a point to check in on Nellie during the first weeks of school but had gotten busy and had not made it down to her room in a few weeks.

Nellie told her, "I so very much appreciate the support you have given me here at AMS. I understand how busy you are with your own students."

Nellie then shared the details of her trip to the teachers' lounge and the comments that had been made about Principal Rookie. As Nellie described the group and their behavior, Sandy just listened and nodded occasionally. She looked concerned, disappointed, but not overly surprised.

Nellie asked, "Why don't I ever see you in the teachers' lounge?"

Sandy Starr responded, "Did you know I used to teach at another school? At the last school district in which I worked, I actually spent time in the teachers' lounge. I would go there during prep time or sometimes eat lunch with other staff members and the principal."

"In that building, the school culture was completely different from that of AMS. Teachers were friendly, supportive, and helpful. The principal had a great relationship with the staff, and I really felt like we were a team. Since that was my first job, I thought all schools operated that way."

She continued, "But when my husband was transferred to this area five years ago, and I was hired at AMS, I soon discovered AMS was quite different. In my first year at AMS, when I would go to the teachers' lounge, the teachers rarely talked about students. When they did, it was in a very negative manner, and they frequently complained about administration. So four and a half years ago, I quit going to the lounge."

Nellie nodded in understanding and said, "I am not at all trying to be negative or critical of Mr. Rookie, but I never see him, and he assigned Ms. Slacker as my mentor. I never see her either."

Sandy Starr shook her head empathetically. She agreed that Nellie deserved more support.

"I heard about the way Mrs. Savage treated you in the office, and I felt for you. I don't know why she is allowed to treat people the way she does; it makes our whole school look bad."

"I feel like she's going to pounce on me and chew my head off my shoulders," said Nellie. "I don't think she likes me."

Sandy continued, "Mr. Rookie is only in his first couple of months as a principal, and hopefully he will be able to get things turned around at AMS. As for Mrs. Savage, Nellie . . . well, that's a bit more complicated." Sandy pursed her lips and shook her head, deciding not to continue with that conversation.

"I'll tell you what," Sandy Starr said. "Why don't you come by my classroom on Friday morning for coffee? A small group of teachers occasionally get together for a coffee klatch. It's fun! We socialize a bit and support each other. Our next meeting is Friday morning in my room at 7:00 a.m. You don't need to bring anything; just tell me what you like to drink in the morning, and I will take care of it."

Nellie smiled. "Thank you. I will! You don't know how much I needed to talk to someone, Sandy. I'll see you on Friday."

The next morning, as Roger entered the building with his morning coffee in hand, he noticed Karl Chameleon meeting with the Bullies in Mildred Morose's classroom. He recalled other times in the past couple weeks that he saw Karl hanging out with the Bullies.

Roger shook his head in amazement that somebody would want to join a negative group like them. As he walked toward his office, he heard loud laughter coming from the Bullies. *They are really having a world of a good time,* he thought.

He was a bit envious that he hadn't laughed like that since becoming principal, yet he knew deep down that theirs was almost certainly at someone else's expense.

Second Faculty Meeting

Roger waited as long as he could, but he had to have another faculty meeting. Mr. Superintendent had directed all building principals to provide meeting minutes to his office quarterly. Admittedly, Roger needed to discuss a few things with his staff—twenty-five (or more) emails he was sending out each day just couldn't cover everything. So he emailed the staff and announced the faculty meeting.

Now he just hoped no one embarrassed him again.

The beginning of the meeting went well. Roger got through all his agenda items without any trouble. He asked if there were any questions or comments before they adjourned. Looking around the room, he saw that Nellie Newcomer had her hand up.

"Yes, Nellie, you have something to share with us?"

Nellie cleared her throat and then said sheepishly, "Well, at a recent meeting in Mrs. Starr's room, we discussed strategies to help our students with homework. Some of our students do not get a lot of support at home, so we were wondering if we could take turns and start an afterschool tutoring program?"

Roger saw Sandy Starr and a handful of other teachers immediately dropped their heads.

Mildred Morose wasted no time, standing abruptly and loudly sharing, "As we are all concerned with the children, we are also concerned with ourselves as a faculty. 'The Union' has worked too hard over the years to get teachers properly compensated for all the extras we do on a weekly basis, and there is no way I am going to provide free teaching. Of course, I cannot control what others of you do with your time."

She then added, swinging her finger back and forth, "Be careful that what you are doing will not set a precedent, because if it does, you'll find yourselves doing it for the rest of your career. Oh, and as this may be helpful in your decision-making, other naïve teachers and principals have tried tutoring in the past. It did not work then, and it will not work now. The real issue that needs to be corrected is parental supervision, not education."

Roger Rookie thanked Mildred Morose for her comment and told Nellie he would consider it. Nellie looked around and realized that, apparently, she had done something wrong. The *Anywhere Way* was talking to her, albeit softly. She already knew Roger's comment meant he was ***not*** going to consider it.

The Principal Survey

School had been in session three months, so Roger Rookie decided it would help him in his professional growth if he surveyed the staff. He knew he was doing a great job helping the school get organized. In a few short months, he had already updated several school documents, including the strategic plan, the annual report, and the student handbook.

Roger knew, however, that he needed improvement in a few areas. He emailed every staff member a link to an online survey and asked them to take five minutes to complete it.

I can't wait to hear what they have to say, he thought. *I'll bet I'm a bit light in knowledge of building and grounds planning. I have not attended too many work sessions on these subjects as of yet.*

It took a few reminders, but after a couple days, all staff members had completed the survey. Roger sat down at his desk and began reviewing the survey results.

He was stunned.

He knew that with an anonymous survey, some staff members might take the opportunity to make critical comments, but it seemed the *entire* staff rated him poorly in almost every category.

Worse, the comments about his lack of leadership were scathing—not only in building management, but also in his instructional leadership and facilitating community resources. Comment after comment complained about his lack of visibility. He wrote the comments that most concerned him in his notebook for further thought.

From my ^Job PERFORMANCE Survey

"Never see the Principal, except during Lunch Duty"

"Too many closed doors, not enough conversations"

"Would like a classroom visit from time to time"

"Wondering what he's doing in his office all the time"

"Never thought I'd work for a celebrity, THE INVISIBLE MAN"

"Who's Roger Rookie?"

Multiple teachers referenced his comment in August about visiting classrooms, and he had not followed through. School climate was another prominent theme mentioned in the survey. The staff clearly felt the school's climate was poor. He jotted down some of these comments as well.

On "CLIMATE"

"Staff and students are never recognized"

"We don't have any fun around here"

"Mr. Rookie never sees us face-to-face, hides behind e-mails"

"The morale sucks! It has hit rock bottom and started to dig"

"Can't quite turn frowns upside down"

"How do we expect scores to improve if there's NO FUN HERE?"

Roger Rookie was speechless. He closed his notebook, tossed his pen, and rubbed his head. *What am I going to do?* he wondered as he closed his office door and headed home.

He reflected on the survey results all weekend. At first he felt defensive, but Roger eventually admitted to himself that the main themes from the survey—and many of the comments—were accurate.

Sitting on the couch with popcorn and soda in hand with late-night TV droning in the background, Roger came to terms with the fact that he had been focusing on the wrong priorities. He truly wanted to make AMS a great school, but he'd been going about it all wrong. *I've been a Hibernator,* Roger concluded. *I have been avoiding what I need to do as a leader to create a better focus on learning.*

Scribbling to himself a few ideas to try, that in hindsight were 20/20, he thought, *Come Monday, things are going to change at Anywhere Middle School.*

THINGS TO DO RIGHT NOW!

1. FOCUS ON CLIMATE

2. NOT HIBERNATE

3. GO SHOPPING FOR LOTS OF FOOD

Roger Rookie's First Makeover: The Hibernator

Teachers' Lounge

"You know how many Rookies it takes to hold a staff meeting?" said Karl Chameleon to his eager audience. "One to email the agenda, another to stand publicly and endure Mildred's spanking machine, and a final one to 'take things under advisement' so he can return to his office and *not* make a decision."

Everyone laughed.

"Hey, c'mon, Chameleon, you're starting to sound like Edgar Sleeper. He's been on a roll with his 'Rookie, the son Neverthere never had' jokes," said Judy Slacker. "Give Rookie a break, the poor thing. He's tuckered out after resting all day in his big chair reading and sending those tiresome emails." She winked and continued. "Imagine how difficult it must be to lug around the large pay increase he received last summer. Almost as difficult as your heavy lifting at the golf course, Chameleon."

"Yeah, OK, OK. Those new oversized drivers are getting a bit heavy in that golf cart," Karl said with a smirk.

"Hey, as far as I'm concerned, there are 365 days in a school year," said Judy Slacker, "and if I'm going to be expected to work more than half of them, I'll be more than happy to enjoy the money that comes along with it," she paused and gave a wicked grin, "or file a grievance and give Rookie a real education about what it's like to run a building."

Laughter again.

"Hey Judy, what are you teaching that new girl you're mentoring," said Mildred Morose.

"Well, just like boot camp, you gotta let the drill sergeant have at her," Judy Slacker replied. "Yep, she's been to Trudy's whipping post a few times so far."

"How's that going for the girl?" someone asked.

"No visible lacerations; just a few internal injuries. It's good for her. Plus a bit fun to watch. We've all been there!"

"Once Rookie gives her about three or four more false promises, we'll let her know how things really work around here."

Mildred added, "I imagine at this point, Sandy Starr is filling her full of a bunch of hearts and smiles. That'll get old. She's new, wet behind the ears.

She'll come around and realize who runs this show. You losers better keep that seat over there warm for her."

Laughter again.

The Coffee Klatch

"How have things wrapped up this quarter, Nellie?" asked Sandy Starr at the following week's coffee klatch. Others had sincere questions to ask Nellie as well.

"Well, I think things are going in the right direction, friends, but to be frank, I'm still a bit unsure if I'm on track with the students. The pacing guide and curriculum map help to a certain degree, but what I really need is a bit more time with Mr. Rookie to see if things are really on track," said Nellie.

"Give him a bit more time, Nellie," Sandy Starr said with reassurance." He's had a very busy start in his first year as a principal. The one thing I have learned in my many years of teaching is that we may not know the pressures others face in their jobs. Regarding his unavailability, I am hoping that this, too, shall pass."

"I try to do that. What I'm concerned about, however, is not simply that I will be evaluated based on my students' performance, but the fact that unless I make a positive difference in their lives, my students will not be ready for high school and college. It's one thing to say I can wait a year or two for good guidance and direction, but my students need good guidance and direction now. That's my biggest worry."

"It is a valid concern, Nellie. We'll continue helping any way we can. Let's hope things improve sooner rather than later. For the most part, I'll be in my classroom, keeping out of the line of fire and doing what I can to help my students. Feel free to visit anytime."

Roger Rookie's Deep Thoughts

As Roger pondered more deeply his recent leadership style and its effects upon others and himself, a few things came to mind in some late-night reflection:

THE HIBERNATOR'S EFFECTS ON STAFF...

SUPERSTARS
- Do not get approval and reinforcement
- Miss interacting with leader
- Feel like they are on an island

FENCESITTERS
- Will blame things in your absence
- Feel uncomfortable making decisions
- Look for leadership in all the wrong places

BULLIES
- Become very powerful
- Complain about your hiding, but actually like it
- Fill the "Leadership Void"

THE HIBERNATOR
continued...

THE LEADER FEELS
- Indecisive
- Afraid
- Powerless

UNINTENDED CONSEQUENCES
- Negative people gain power
- Good people lose confidence
- Leader is unaware of what is happening in the school

Chapter 3
Roger Rookie's Next Makeover: The Glad-Hander

Roger scheduled a faculty meeting for Monday morning at 7:30. He was determined to learn from the survey results. As Roger walked into the faculty meeting, his last thought was, *I am going to change the climate in this building. That'll help learning! I just know I'm onto something. I'll find that path! Let the secret be revealed!*

As teachers filed into the teachers' lounge, they were surprised to see an assortment of bagels, muffins, juice, and coffee. Roger began the meeting by thanking the staff for taking the time to complete his survey.

Roger then said, "I want to apologize. The first quarter of the school year I have been busy, but I chose to focus my energy on the wrong things. I avoided some things on which I should have focused more. I need to focus more on you all. School climate is *numero uno* in importance, as I've learned. Beginning today, I am committed to visiting classrooms and recognizing our students and staff for the great things you do. We are going to start having some fun around here."

Immediately, Nellie Newcomer, Sandy Starr, and others looked uncomfortable.

The Bullies appeared ready to complain, but to Roger's pleasant surprise, they did not say anything; they just kept filling their faces with treats and talking with one another. Roger finished the meeting by thanking the staff for their hard work.

Roger thought to himself, *Man, when I look in the mirror, I am looking at one smart cat! If the teachers have food in their mouths, it's tough for them to complain. It may cost me a little scratch, but that new Big-Box Retailer in town is going to be my new best friend. I'm buying in bulk!*

The first two weeks after the meeting, Roger Rookie kept his word and visited classrooms every day. He was surprised to learn how good some of the AMS teachers were. Some of their lessons were a bit lacking in delivery, but with a little help, these teachers could be fantastic. He also visited a few classrooms where teachers consistently performed below standard. Roger knew he would never put his own children in those classrooms. Well, when he had children, anyway. First things first. . .

Roger knew he needed to start developing positive relationships with students and parents. Although an email or a "form" letter would have been more efficient, Roger instead spent time in the evening writing personal notes to students for improving their grades or behavior.

I've got to start connecting with every student and family, he decided. *I just know the secret to improved learning is taking care of people!*

He wrote note after note to staff members when he saw creative lessons in their classrooms. Roger made a point to write a personal note to every teacher.

I've got to make sure each note is unique so I am praising them for specific actions, Roger thought to himself.

Roger also sent notes to parents, acknowledging their students' improvement or for their support of the school. Suddenly he was incredibly busy, but since he had started visiting classrooms and recognizing people for positive performance or behavior, he liked his job more.

Seminar Problem

One day after school, Roger returned to his office and saw a handful of teachers waiting for him in his office. He took one look at the faces of the group and knew he was in trouble.

Oh, no! Mildred Morose and Judy Slacker. This isn't going to be a party!

This group of teachers had already distinguished themselves for finding innovative ways to spend *less* time with students. *Could that be what this impromptu meeting is all about?* he wondered.

Roger welcomed the group, exchanged a few pleasantries, and asked the teachers what they wished to discuss.

Mildred Morose responded, "Mr. Rookie, our representative faculty group would like to discuss Seminar, our school's advisor/advisee time."

Roger wondered whom they actually represented but cautioned himself against taking that route.

She continued, "As you know, Seminar was extended five minutes by your predecessor, Mr. Neverthere, without any input from teachers. What I am sure he did not realize was that our lunch break was reduced from thirty-five to thirty minutes. To compound the problem, this is the worst-behaved bunch of malcontents we have ever had at AMS. We need recuperation time. Trudy Savage warned us of the trouble this year's students would be after meeting the parents at summer registration."

Judy Slacker added, "Might a better approach be that paraprofessionals cover lunch? In doing so, Seminar could revert back to being five fewer minutes."

Roger was surprised that five minutes of lunchtime was an issue.

Ned Neverthere had told Roger when he first arrived that Seminar had been implemented to help students build a relationship with the faculty during their years at AMS. It also was a structured setting that helped students stay organized with their homework.

Roger thought, *I remember Mr. Neverthere saying also that several teachers, his superstar teachers, had complained they could use more Seminar time to help students, so he added another five minutes.*

Roger didn't share this with the group.

Roger assured the group he would try to find a solution.

"Thank you, Mr. Rookie," said Mildred Morose on behalf of the group. "We trust you will do the right thing."

They left for the lounge.

Roger thought about the group's request and, at the same time, mulled over his charge to improve a focus on learning at Anywhere Middle School.

In revisiting his old *How to Be a Good School Principal* textbook late at night, with popcorn and soda pop as usual, Roger began jotting down some notes on what a focus on learning would look like. He had noted that. . .

A FOCUS ON <u>LEARNING</u>

* Would affect the way business is done around here;

* Would involve changes in behaviors, beliefs, and values;

* Would change the personality of Anywhere.

EYE ON
THE BALL

LEARNING

He studied his notes and scratched out a few drawings of flow charts and other things that would potentially impact a focus on learning. He reflected on the first quarter and how he hadn't come out of his office much. He munched and doodled as he thought about what needed to change.

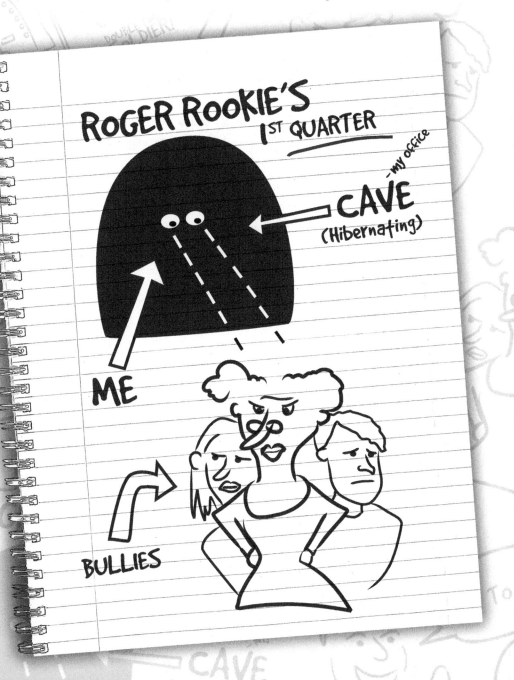

Roger pondered, *During the first quarter, I certainly got to know the way business was done around here, and I didn't like it. If behaviors and beliefs are any indication, I can see why my superintendent wants things changed. Too bad I spent nine weeks accepting things as they were. As principal, I gotta get something done.*

His thoughts wandered to Nellie. *Not sure who is helping Nellie, if anyone, but I feel bad that I assigned Judy Slacker as her mentor. I knew that was wrong in the first place. Stupid move! Back to my marching orders . . . just how can I move learning in a direction I want it to go?*

Roger thought of the initial success in his newfound overtures at building better relationships. He remembered the old adage: *The way to a person's heart is through one's appetite.*

He surmised, *I just need to keep this ship sailing on the climate thing. If I make it my mission to cater to the people every day, folks will love coming to work because they'll feel good. This'll motivate them to do the right thing by kids, won't it?*

He took another bite of popcorn and continued sketching his thoughts.

WAY TO GO!
WOULD YOU LIKE FRIES WITH THAT?
PRINCIPAL
E=MC²
I'll bet THIS is THE SECRET!
YOUR MARCHING ORDERS...
DOUBLE TIME SOLDIER!
ME
CAVE (Hibernating)
PRINCIPAL

Yep, same to 'em but more of it. Climate. It's the path! I'll do my darnedest to have the best school climate ever! If people LOVE working for me, and if they actually like me, I'll bet we start making an impact on this learning thing.

If people are happier, aren't they more productive? That'll take care of the test scores. Boy, wouldn't that make my superintendent happy? Carol Charming would even write about it. I'd be a hero!

In the days and weeks that followed, Roger Rookie doubled down on climate, and, to be sure, climate was improving. He wrote positive notes, visited classrooms, observed lessons, and, sure, all this attention to people gave him longer hours at work, once everyone went home. He took home paperwork and wrote notes over snacks and late-night television. Things weren't all that bad.

Rookie-isms

With the climate slowly beginning to improve in the school, Roger Rookie did not want this Seminar issue to upset staff. It appeared nobody liked former principal Ned Neverthere, and Roger was determined to get the staff to like him.

Roger thought, *This is a tough group to win over. Maybe if I "give" on this issue, the staff might give me a break on something later, especially if they see me as being on their side as the principal.*

Roger henceforth announced that Seminar would be reduced by five minutes. A couple of the teachers personally thanked Roger for respecting them and finding such a great solution. They then headed to the lounge.

One of the changes Roger committed to as part of his climate-change initiative was meeting regularly with new staff members, so he scheduled a meeting with Nellie to see how her first year was going. Nellie's excitement and love of teaching was evident as she described how lucky and honored she felt to be teaching at AMS. Roger probed a little deeper, and Nellie shared some struggles she was having with a few students. When Roger heard the student names, he was not surprised, as those students were challenges for almost the entire staff.

Roger asked Nellie, "How have your conversations been going between you and your mentor, Judy Slacker?"

He noticed the immediate change in her expression.

"Unfortunately, I only met with Ms. Slacker once during the August workshop before school had started."

"Oh . . . that's not good, Nellie," Roger said. "I'll speak with Ms. Slacker and encourage her to schedule bi-weekly meetings with you. I really want her to serve as a better resource for you."

Roger finished up the meeting and walked out, knowing his decision to allow Judy Slacker to be anyone's mentor was a mistake. He felt like a heel and knew he should meet with Judy and be specific about her role as a mentor.

Roger Rookie never met with Judy Slacker; instead, he sent the following email to the entire staff:

Faculty Colleagues:

Thank you for your efforts in serving students thus far this year. As a gentle reminder to all, will you please take some of your valuable time and ensure that every so often, you stop by the classrooms of our newer staff members to offer them the support, advice, and encouragement valued as members of our school family. I trust all is well with you and that you will support our new faculty in their launch of professional careers.

Warm regards,

Mr. Rookie

"Warm regards? School family?! *HA!*" said Judy Slacker, sitting next to Edgar Sleeper, Mildred Morose, and Karl Chameleon in the teachers' lounge. "Gag me with the pointed end of a hot charcoal poker! Do you think we're doing these newbies any favors by coddling them with group hugs? We'll leave that to Sandy Starr."

"If anything, they need to toughen up a bit," Edgar said. "A good dose of 'tough love' is probably better for them, 'cause if they steel their resolve quickly, they'll be much better off in the long run. These kids aren't getting any easier to educate. And don't even get me started on the parents!"

Karl Chameleon nodded in agreement.

"I deleted the email as soon as I saw the source," said Mildred Morose. "I have no time for Rookie-isms. Other things need my attention, like my knitting. What did it say?"

The only people who were influenced by Roger Rookie's email were AMS's superstars. Although they had done a great job of helping new staff, they felt guilty for not having done more. It certainly did not change behavior with those who needed it. And neither the negligence of the Bullies nor the guilt of the Superstars helped Nellie and the other new teachers at AMS.

Following the Agenda

As part of his personal improvement plan that he reported to his superintendent, Roger Rookie had determined the school needed monthly faculty meetings to stay organized. He also started putting the agenda out to all staff members several days prior to the meeting and asked staff to add any items to the agenda they wished to discuss.

Roger didn't care who offered up items or how many there were, as his new strategy of "All-You-Can-Eat Breakfast Buffet" was significantly reducing the number of complaints at meetings. But it seemed the direction of conversation was getting away from him.

His first new agenda item at the faculty meetings was "Positive Comments."

Roger had gotten in the habit of using specific praise to point out extraordinary performance by teachers and anonymous praise (sometimes made up) about observing a "teacher" doing something remarkable with students.

He said, "Last week I had the opportunity to walk by a classroom and spent a few minutes with rapt attention to the high interest and engagement of students in hearing how their academic learning was to make a difference in their lives. To have faculty members with such a command of their subject matter and the best interest of students is quite humbling, for sure. Thank you for that opportunity as your leader!"

He saw Karl Chameleon smile, look at Edgar Sleeper, and then point to himself. Edgar shook his head, in friendly banter, and pointed back at himself. Roger loved using anonymous praise because every time he used it, he could tell several teachers thought he was specifically talking about them.

Roger hoped the combination of free food and positive comments would put teachers in a good mood so that he could have a meeting without controversy.

The meeting had been going well. Roger was able to get through most of the agenda with few questions or comments. With the finish line in sight, he was about to adjourn the meeting when he looked up and saw Mildred Morose trying to catch his eye.

Roger wondered why Mildred was actually behaving civilly and raising her hand when she normally just rudely interrupted him.

Reluctantly, Roger said, "Yes, Mrs. Morose, what is on your mind?"

Mildred stood up, cleared her throat and in a completely fake voice that she must have thought made her sound like a pleasant person, asked, "May we please have a conversation on why the school couldn't use paraprofessionals to cover the before-school duty?"

She continued before Roger responded, positioning herself upright for greater visibility, "As you know, Mr. Rookie, we teachers serve a fifteen-minute, six-week supervision of the commons area before students are dismissed to their first class. You, of all people, know how big our class sizes are this year. If we want any chance of raising test scores, which seems to be so important to Central Office, we need more time to prepare for this group of monsters."

The "monsters" comment got a laugh out of the usual cast of malcontents.

Edgar Sleeper then jumped in the fracas. "Mr. Rookie, the staff is still so grateful to you for using paraprofessionals to cover the lunch line, wouldn't it make sense to also use paraprofessionals to cover the before-school duty? We took a poll and have found that most faculty would concur."

A poll, Roger thought. *I'm not a fan of these polls.*

Judy Slacker and LaVon Babble were nodding in agreement, and Roger noticed several others joining them. As Roger looked around the room, he also noticed some of his best teachers could not look him in the eyes; they had their heads down.

Roger did not know what to do. He didn't want conflict or pushback, so he told the group he would consider their request. *I wonder if more paraprofessional supervision would help their mood and the school climate,* he pondered.

Phoning a Friend

Roger phoned a friend for advice. He called his old college buddy, Joel Gerrymander, who was in his third year as a principal/athletic director.

Truth be told, Roger thought, *this guy plays a bit fast and loose with his job, but he's a friend who will surely give me ten minutes of conversation and a straight answer, like it or not.*

Joel answered his call enthusiastically, "Dude! What's happening? I hear you got the big chair now. Oh, just one second, text incoming!"

Roger heard the telephone drop as Joel Gerrymander answered the text.

"Ok, Rog, I'm back. Whazzzz UP?"

"Great to hear your voice, Joel. Yes, I took over for Ned Neverthere and have my superintendent breathing down my neck to make our school more focused on learning. You know, Joel, I have a situation I'd like to discuss if you don't mind taking just a few minutes."

"Of course not. Shoot!" said Joel with quick interest.

Roger shared the faculty meeting concern from the Bullies. Joel listened as best he could while shooting Nerf hoops and slamming an energy drink. He agreed with Roger that the teachers should have spoken about this "poll thing" with him prior to the meeting.

"These poll stunts are a pain, dude," Joel agreed. "I've got to ask you though, Roger: How's it working for you, letting anyone in the building suggest things for your staff meeting agendas? Think about this: You have Sweet Polly Purebred on one side of the faculty meeting and Eddie Haskell on the other. Dude—you gonna trust them equally?! For instance, when I involve a committee in making decisions, I tell my coaches, 'You *advise*, then *I* make the final decisions myself. Period.'

"What I do, Rog, is define the boundaries of conversation, and if I don't like 'em, I redefine 'em to my advantage. It gets a bit political at times, but hey, this is a political game we're in. I certainly don't let teachers re-ink the boundaries on *anything*. That just doesn't work."

"I guess that makes sense," Roger said. "I admit, Joel, I'm getting a bit worried because my next report to the superintendent is due quite soon. I think the school board is going to have its way with him if he can't serve up something new and nifty on improved learning soon."

"Roger, dude, don't you see that if you lie belly-up on this para-pro issue, the staff will have a list of others they want changed?"

"I'm hoping, Joel, that if I cover this particular duty with paraprofessionals, I may be able to ask the teachers to give on other issues."

"Yeah . . . when I'm wearing a speedo while snowmobiling and whistling Dixie, that'll happen! Hey, I don't mean to be negative. Maybe you can make it work; you're a more popular guy than I. Good luck to you, dude! Remember, Rog: *boundaries*. Gotta run!"

Roger thanked Joel Gerrymander for listening. He knew before he called Joel what he was going to do, and he was hoping Joel would affirm his decision. From the tone of the conversation, Roger knew that Joel, in fact, did not support caving in to the staff, but rationalized that Joel had no idea how tough the situation was and how difficult it was telling this staff no.

Belly Up

Later in the week, Roger emailed the staff that he would be able to use paraprofessionals to cover the before-school duty. He was a same-day rock star, receiving some nice emails, a couple of high fives, and even a plate of cookies.

That will go great with my popcorn this evening, Roger thought. *Some days, it really is great being the principal.*

Over popcorn and soda pop that evening, Roger's thoughts wandered as he continued thinking about the secret to a better path to a school-wide focus on learning.

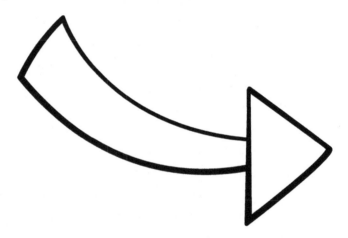

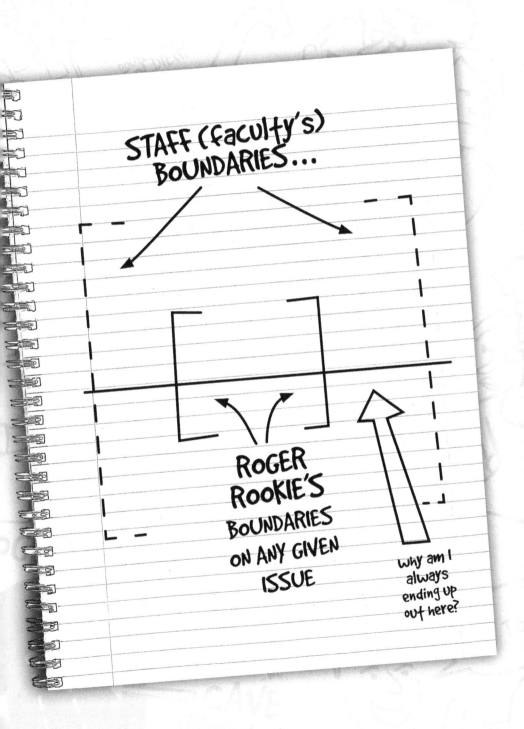

The following week, Karl Chameleon stopped into Roger's office.

"Hey, Mr. Rookie, do you have time to meet?"

"Always, Karl."

Roger asked Karl how everything was going and complimented him on his classroom. Karl exchanged pleasantries and got right down to business.

"Mr. Rookie, the math department is going to begin its graphing unit next month. We were hoping you would be able to support the math department by purchasing new graphing calculators."

Karl was quick to mention they would not order a calculator for each student; instead, they would save money by only ordering a few classroom sets that could be shared.

"What's the price tag, Karl?" Roger asked.

Karl Chameleon smiled and produced three separate quotes he had already worked on. The cheapest quote for the required number of calculators was $2,343.00. Roger thanked Karl for stopping in and doing the legwork on getting quotes for the calculators.

"What I'll do, Karl, is consider this request and get back with you and the department very soon."

When Karl Chameleon heard those words, he knew he was in trouble.

Pointing the Finger at Others

The next morning, Roger Rookie stopped in Karl Chameleon's room before school.

"Karl, I very much understand your need for calculators, but this one's a bit out of my hands, I admit. You know the crew from Central Office that I answer to. They're not going to budge and spend even one nickel more than what they budgeted for AMS."

He added, "If it were my decision, Karl, we would get you those calculators. I know what a great teacher you are, and this is a reasonable request. However, Central Office is instead forcing me to make budget reductions, and purchasing the calculators can't happen with those marching orders. I'm very sorry, but this is our reality for this year."

Karl Chameleon was disappointed but thanked Roger Rookie for meeting with him and telling him face-to-face. He then ran to the teachers' lounge to share the news of how Central Office did not support the hard-working staff at AMS.

This would not be the last time Roger blamed others for decisions.

Unintentional Consequences

Nellie Newcomer was flustered as she entered Sandy Starr's room.

"Hi, Nellie," Sandy said.

"Hi, Sandy. Do you have any ideas on how I can keep up with my struggling students when I'm no longer assigned to them in the morning? Now that they're all in the cafeteria instead of our classrooms, I'm not able to help them as well when I see they're falling behind."

"It frustrates me as well, Nellie. Have you thought about asking them down?"

"Yes, I've already done that, but they don't want to come. Evidently they are allowed to sleep after arriving, which I don't believe is what was intended."

"Not intended, Nellie . . . but predictable, I'm sad to say."

Boundaries and Bullets

Roger read an article from his Principals Association Newsletter that talked about boosting morale through site-based management. He thought, *What a great way to move forward with a positive climate! I'll form a site-based decision-making committee. Staff will love it!*

Roger had served on a building advisory as a teacher and really enjoyed having a voice in school decision-making. At that time, he'd had several ideas he thought would help more students experience success. He believed in shared leadership. Maybe he could work with his staff and implement some at Anywhere Middle School.

He emailed the staff, asking for teacher volunteers to serve on the site-based decision-making committee. Roger was excited, yet a bit shocked, when by the end of the day, eight teachers had indicated their interest in serving on the committee.

Bonus! he thought.

Roger then saw the list of names, none of whom Roger would have thought would volunteer extra time; in fact, three of the Bullies, Mildred Morose, Judy Slacker, and Edgar Sleeper, asked to be on the committee. Roger also noticed that none of his most effective teachers had signed up.

Gosh! I was really hoping for Sandy Starr; even Karl Chameleon would be better than these folks, he grimaced.

Roger Rookie scheduled the first meeting. His main agenda item was increasing the communication between teachers and parents. Although he and a few other teachers contacted parents on a regular basis, the majority of AMS staff did not contact parents until there was a problem. And then they would request that the principal do it! Roger wanted to take a proactive approach, and he believed the first contact from school should be on a positive note, no matter the student—and no matter the parent.

"What do you mean, contact the parent when there's **not** a problem?" Mildred Morose balked. "The idea will not work. Positive support efforts have been tried and have not worked either. Plus, Roger, as we're sure you would agree, teachers are already overworked and underpaid."

Judy Slacker blurted out, "Until we change our students' parents, it does not matter what we do; some kids are just not going to get it."

Roger looked around the room in disbelief.

Mildred Morose then said, "I think I do have an option for us to consider that would make inroads to positive direction on this. Why don't we vote to give teachers additional planning time?"

Roger wanted to dodge this whole notion of voting on anything, as that was never his intention with the committee. *What's going on here?*

How did the meeting shift in this direction? he wondered. He needed to react quickly.

"Mrs. Morose, will you work with others on this committee and provide me with a detailed proposal?"

She smiled; the rest of the committee nodded, and Mildred Morose said, "We'll get right to work on this, Mr. Rookie."

Dodged that bullet, Roger thought.

The rest of the meeting was spent discussing concerns teachers had about students or procedures. Roger's committee had turned into a complaint department. Rather than making positive strides for school improvement, he was sitting and listening to folks who were unhappy with their jobs (and lives).

Roger Rookie left the meeting discouraged and wondered why he'd ever formed a site-based decision-making committee. His only consolation was that Christmas break would start in a few days, and he would have a two-week break.

Last Day before Break

Anywhere Middle School always dismissed children right after lunch on the last day before holiday break. As staff gathered for their afternoon holiday party, Roger Rookie thought of the large amount of money he had spent for gifts that he wrapped for a game in which faculty drew names and selected presents from a table, those later in the drawing able to steal from others who had drawn before.

Anywhere's paraprofessionals arrived a bit later than the rest of the staff and were all sitting together in the group, not appearing to have much of a good time. *Holidays aren't happy for everyone,* Roger thought to himself sadly. *Maybe this game will pick up their spirits.*

Teachers seem to be enjoying it for the most part, Roger mused, yet his mind wandered . . .

It's probably bad to think about this, but it feels as though I'm giving, giving, and giving, and those who don't give too awful much are taking, taking, and taking. The more presents I dole out, the more it seems I'm expected to be Santa Claus. I love the positive atmosphere; the climate around here is most certainly better than when I came. But I'm wondering when we'll start turning the corner on some of these things that will truly improve learning at our school.

I'm beginning to wonder if what I'm doing is the secret solution, after all.

"Merry Christmas, everyone, and a Happy New Year," Roger said as the gifts were opened.

"Come on! A stupid candle?" Mildred Morose whispered.

"Cool! A coffee mug for my deer blind," Karl Chameleon said.

"Merry Christmas, Nellie! We're so glad you're with us," said Sandy Starr.

"Yeah—to take some of the load off the rest of us," chimed Judy Slacker.

Roger concluded the gathering by saying, "Enjoy your time with family, and I look forward to your return after your most-deserved time with loved ones and the holidays."

As he munched on holiday-flavored popcorn and drank eggnog-flavored soda pop that evening, Roger's thoughts again went back to his search for the secret of a focus on school-wide learning.

Back at It

Roger returned from the two-week Christmas break ready to go, working even harder to win over the staff. The time away had recharged his batteries, and he was fired up to maintain the positive momentum at AMS. Roger continued to be visible in classrooms and kept writing notes to students, staff, and parents. He noticed a few other teachers writing personal notes to students and parents too.

School had been back in session a few days when Roger headed into school early to get some work done before staff and students arrived. Roger was halfway through his first cup of coffee when Mildred Morose walked in. His rejuvenated spirit quickly left his body; he tried hard not to let it show.

"Hello, Mrs. Morose, so very nice to see you . . . so early in the morning."

Mildred used her fake nice voice to greet him. Roger played along. After exchanging fake interest in each other's holiday breaks, Mildred stated, "Mr. Rookie, don't you think it is time to discuss my proposal, uh, I mean, the leadership team's proposal for additional planning time so departments could review data and plan interdisciplinary units?"

Roger did not believe for a minute that Mildred Morose was concerned with planning time or data; this was just another ploy of Mildred's to spend less time with students. Instead of being honest with Mildred and telling her he thought time was better spent instructing students, Roger said, "Mrs. Morose, your timing is well-placed on this cordial visit, but I regret to inform you the 'higher ups' have denied this request."

Mildred shook her head, making several negative comments about the Central Office staff. "I have half a mind to get a petition started to throw the bum-of-a-superintendent out of his office," she snarled. "Please understand I say this in no way representing the views of the committee and, of course, with no disrespect to you, sir," she feigned.

Roger listened to her noxious comments. He felt guilty and disloyal for having created the problem. He hoped the whole notion of a petition was just posturing and venom. He worried deep down about being "found out."

Checking on the Newbie

Roger scheduled another meeting with Nellie Newcomer. He had noticed during walk-throughs that, although her lessons were creative, and students appeared engaged, Nellie seemed not quite her usual, perky self. When Roger entered her room, he could not help but be impressed with how organized she was. Nellie Newcomer used her limited square footage as well as the most veteran teachers in the district. He sat in a student desk next to Nellie's.

"How are things going for you, Nellie?" he asked.

"Christmas break helped recharge my batteries, Mr. Rookie, and I believe I am ready for the second semester. Please offer me any advice you can provide, as I would very much appreciate it."

Nellie had learned a lot her first semester about working with students and the challenges of trying to help every student be successful. She was a very popular teacher, although some students took advantage of her kindness from time to time. As she was a "newbie," they were able to pull the wool over her eyes here and there, but she was a quick learner.

Roger asked, "What's been your relationship with the other staff members, Nellie? Are you finding the 'fit' and professional family we all desire?"

Nellie responded, "Mrs. Starr and a small group of teachers have really been helpful in coaching me in the school routines and offering me strategies to help struggling learners."

Roger agreed with Nellie and said that Sandy was a great role model for all educators. "How about Ms. Slacker?" he inquired.

Nellie looked at Roger and said in a matter-of-fact manner, "Ms. Slacker has not met with me since long before Christmas; we really don't have a relationship. Whenever I need help, I ask other teachers whom I've gotten to know and trust."

Nellie then looked at Roger and said in a very quiet voice, "Mr. Rookie, please forgive me for saying this, but Ms. Slacker should never again be allowed to be a mentor. She has never appeared to care about me, and from what I've witnessed so far, she is not somebody I would ever want to use as a role model."

Roger Rookie had a big lump in his throat. He told Nellie, "I'm very sorry you have not had a good experience with Ms. Slacker, and I'm glad you've connected with teachers like Mrs. Starr."

As Roger walked out of the room and grimaced at the thought of allowing Judy Slacker to be a mentor, he thought to himself, *Nellie was a first-year teacher who needed support and deserved better. I have nobody to blame but myself, especially since I didn't even speak with Judy about her responsibilities as a mentor like I told Nellie I would. I'm sitting here searching for the secret to better student learning, and it seems at times I'm keeping a secret from myself: Glad-handing and over-adapting to others won't make our problems go away or get better. I feel like such a heel.*

Despite these apprehensions, Roger did believe the school had turned a corner with climate. He was hoping a new way of doing business and getting along with each other made at least a small difference. *It is tiring, though. Some nights, I just can't believe how quickly I crash when I get home,* Roger admitted to himself.

On the bright side, students, teachers, staff members and parents appeared to be happy with AMS. The school had a more positive environment; however, Roger knew they were still falling short regarding test scores. The school's student achievement data showed that many students were not performing at grade level, and AMS data was lower than most of the schools in the entire district.

At the end of the day, I just know I'm going to be on the hook for these test scores, thought Roger. *It seems like I'm climbing the steps to success as fast as I can and even bringing lots of folks with me. They're happy; they like me. I'm in their classes, making lots of positive calls home on the teachers' behalf, and I'm even welcome in the lounge, at times. I just wonder if I'm on the right stairway.*

Mid-Year Evaluation

Roger waited anxiously for a meeting with Mr. Superintendent. It was his mid-year evaluation, and nerves had his stomach in knots. A report on AMS's focus on school-wide learning was to be part of the discussion, as was his plan for the upcoming month of high-stakes tests.

Those are the test scores Carol Charming never forgets about, he worried.

Fidgeting with his folder and pen—and doodling feverishly—he could not help but garner the attention of Cindy Sage, Mr. Superintendent's secretary, who sat outside his office.

Cindy had been serving superintendents in the district for over thirty years. She was a local girl, born and raised, married to a traveling executive who showed few signs of slowing down in his own career. Cindy Sage was on her fourth superintendent and planned to retire in a few years when her last child was out of college. She was a quiet, meticulous, loyal administrative professional with deep knowledge of the district and an understanding of its happenings.

She very much liked Roger Rookie, as he reminded her of one of her sons. She had four.

"Roger, Mr. Superintendent is taking calls regarding last night's board meeting, and it looks as if it will be another fifteen to twenty minutes. Can I get you a cup of coffee?"

"No thank you, ma'am. I appreciate it, though."

She watched as he doodled more nervously in his scratch pad.

"Roger, why don't you come sit in the lounge area with me. I have a few minutes, and I would like to talk. Would you mind?"

"Well, I guess not. That would be nice," he said, happy to have a distraction. As they walked to the lounge area, he said, "Every time I stop in, it seems we're always so busy."

Upon sitting down in the lounge's plush chairs, she said inquisitively, "Please tell me how things are going, Roger. I once was a student at AMS. I have known every teacher and principal in that building for the past thirty years, and I have been quite interested in how you would do in the post-Neverthere era." She chuckled. As an afterthought she added, "Ned Neverthere, that old fella. Did you know he and I graduated together from high school, Roger?"

"No, ma'am. It's a small world, isn't it?"

"It sure is, Roger. You seem to be handling yourself well at AMS, but between you and me, I figured it was going to be a bit rough on you at first."

"Why's that, Mrs. Sage?"

"Ned Neverthere didn't exactly leave you with a well-oiled machine. What once was the shiniest star in the district—Ned's leadership, that is—lost a bit of its luster near the end. Now I adore Ned, so I'll say no more, but the focus on learning did slip away from him, and it seems as though it is a pretty tough nut to crack at this point."

"Glad to hear someone realizes it, ma'am. I'm trying hard to turn things around, but I'm thinking it may take a bit more time than my boss is going to allow."

"Does that have you worried, Roger?"

"Yeah, a bit. But I'm an optimist. I'm working on figuring out the secret to this whole thing, and I hope I'm on the right path."

"Would you like to share? With thirty years in this office, having put four boys and a girl through the school system, and watching my share of principals wield their leadership with hundreds of staff and thousands of students, I might be able to give you a good, honest perspective. I'll probably learn a bit from what you've done, too."

"Thanks for asking. Do we have about ten minutes or so?"

"I'll bet we still have another fifteen or twenty," Cindy said.

"Here goes."

Roger shared with Cindy Sage some of what was going on at Anywhere Middle School. She listened intently as he talked about his struggles getting the staff to embrace changes he felt would be beneficial for students. Cindy did not ask a lot of questions but listened actively. Roger avoided mentioning some of the changes he had made to appease the teachers, but Cindy had seen too many new principals not to know the dynamics of what probably went on. To Roger's surprise, once he finally shared with Cindy all the stuff he had tried in an effort to shift to a focus on learning rather than on teaching, he actually felt good about getting it off his shoulders.

"Roger, I want you to know that your confidence placed in me is admirable," she said. Roger knew one of Cindy's best qualities was her ability to listen without judging. She also had a great way of asking questions that could lead a person to finding his or her own solution. She started with her first question: "Roger, if you could wave a magic wand, what would your perfect school look like?"

Roger didn't have to think up an answer; he knew exactly what he wanted. "I want a school that, when you walk into it, you know it is a place you *want* your son or daughter to attend. I want a school where staff members collaborate and work as a team and where the focus of meetings and professional development is on how the school can improve so every student learns and develops to his or her potential."

"What do you believe, Roger, is preventing AMS from being that school?"

"Teachers, it seems, especially the building leadership team, continually take exception to every idea that requires teachers to teach differently," he responded. "It seems as if AMS is more about meeting the *wants* of teachers than it is about meeting the needs of students. Now don't get me wrong, Mrs. Sage, I am working on this, and I think I'm figuring out the secret. But it's taking just a bit more time than I thought it would."

"Sounds challenging, indeed, Roger."

Roger feigned optimism when he said, "I have made some huge moves toward better relationships, which are positioning us to head in the right direction. I'm hoping the boss will concur that these changes have been beneficial."

He trusted Cindy Sage, but at the same time realized she was his boss' confidential secretary. Keeping that in mind, he didn't want to let too much out of the bag. He thought of the Bullies and their leader, Mildred Morose, and of how he would get nervous before faculty meetings because of this group. He thought also of Mildred's rude behavior. He thought of all the time he spent each day mired in minutia in an attempt to keep staff happy. He thought about how much time this was taking away from moving the students forward academically.

Roger then thought of his secretary, Trudy Savage, and her behavior and the negative impact it had on AMS. He thought about his attempts at trying to change Trudy Savage's behavior by "killing her with kindness" and about how desperately he had hoped his positive attitude would rub off on her.

He thought that, although the building climate was 100 percent better than when he arrived (in fact, several teachers had shared that they liked the new atmosphere), in other areas the school was a long way from what he had hoped for. He thought about . . .

"Roger . . . Roger . . . are you still with me?" Cindy said with a warm smile.

"Yes, ma'am," Roger said. He realized he had been lost in thought—thoughts he wasn't prepared to share.

"You must have a lot on your mind, Roger. That's natural for one assuming so much leadership responsibility so early in one's career." She then asked, "How many teacher evaluations have you done, Roger?"

Roger thought for a moment and said, "Mrs. Sage, I have completed about six, with another six to do on this year's rotation."

"It might not be my business to pry, Roger, but were any of the evaluations with teachers who are not helping you create the ideal school you described earlier?"

Roger felt himself tense up knowing the answer was yes. He was too embarrassed to admit that he had been overly positive in his evaluations and had not given the teachers constructive feedback and actions to improve instruction at AMS. Rather than answer, he gave a noncommittal shrug.

"How are your new teachers doing? And, more importantly, Roger, are they eating lunch with the right people?"

To this, Roger answered, "Very well, thank you. And yes, Nellie Newcomer, for one, is spending a lot of time with Sandy Starr." Roger did not mention whom he assigned as a mentor.

"That's excellent news," Cindy replied. She waited a few beats before speaking again because she could see Roger was deep in thought.

What an idiot I have been allowing the most negative teachers to serve as mentors instead of assuring that our best teachers match up well with new hires, he pondered.

"Roger, you know best what the *real* strengths, weaknesses, and opportunities are at Anywhere Middle School. It is not going to take your superintendent or your mid-year evaluation to sort these out. I think you have done a bit of this today while sitting here with me," Cindy said. "And for what it is worth, I believe you have within you the ability and the smarts to take Anywhere Middle School from where it is now to that 'better place' you described to me just a few minutes ago."

"Thank you, Mrs. Sage. It means a lot that you have such confidence in me. I'm not going to let anyone down. We'll move this place forward, that's for sure."

Roger could hear Mr. Superintendent wrapping up his phone call in the other room. *I have an opinion to what the problem is at AMS,* he thought while he waited for his boss to call him. *The problem with Anywhere Middle School is the students and staff need a strong leader, somebody willing to get the right stakeholders working toward a shared vision. The staff needs a leader who knows his core values and always puts the needs of students ahead of the wants of staff. A leader can never blame the higher-ups for something he's gutless to do. My actions of late have suggested I am more interested in making friends than being a true leader. That's no way to improve learning. That's simply a way to share smiles and still end up getting stabbed in the back. I have been keeping a secret from myself: A leader needs to hold others accountable as well as himself.*

Roger appreciated Cindy Sage's kind words and her calm reassurance and confidence in him. Without scolding him, she had helped him realize he needed to grow up, put on his big-boy pants, and find the secret that had been eluding him. In his determination *not* to act like Ned Neverthere, he had instead become a cheerleader, trying to be everyone's friend at the expense of helping children succeed. The teachers liked Roger Rookie, but Roger was pretty sure most folks did not respect him.

That weekend, he reflected on his actions over the previous few months. He was so focused on trying to get people to like him that he lost focus of why he had become an administrator: to make a difference for students and staff. Roger had to rethink his leadership style in finding the secret solution, his pathway to leadership success.

Teachers' Lounge

"Hey Babble, we hear Rookie is coming in to do your evaluation next week," Mildred Morose said. "What sort of a dog and pony show do you have planned for the boy?"

"Nothing much, Mildred. Like you think *any* of us are going to get a bad evaluation? We were here long before Rookie took off his training wheels, and we'll be here long after he leaves, which by my estimation is roughly 110 days away."

Laughter filtered throughout the room.

"Hey, did you hear how many principals it takes to form a building-leadership committee?" Karl asked.

"Oh, come on Chameleon; don't quit your day job!"

"Three. One to write up an agenda we'll choose to ignore. Another to take two weeks to make the decision Mildred wants anyway. And a third to miss the fact that by the time we negotiate our next contract, we'll all be getting paid a stipend to spend our time *serving* on that site-based decision-making committee!"

At that, the room filled again with laughter.

"Hey, any luck with your calculators, you doorknob?" said Mildred.

"C'mon guys; give me time. I'll be golfing with someone from Central Office at the Athletic League Scramble, and I'll find out who's telling Rookie no."

"Where's Judy Slacker today?"

"She left early again. Something about a very important meeting at the department store."

Laughter.

"Hey, staff meeting tomorrow morning. Rise and shine early, my fellow fools! Lounge bet: How many think our resident goodie-two-shoes combo, Sandy and our new 'Sandy Jr.,' will sit again in the front row, sucking up as usual?"

"Darn well better have a bit more variety on the menu," said Mildred Morose. "Otherwise, we'll have to give Rookie a bit of a tune-up as to the lifestyle we are accustomed to living around here."

More laughter.

The Coffee Klatch

"I feel so much better about my mid-year evaluation, Mrs. Starr," said Nellie Newcomer. "Mr. Rookie gave me quite high marks for planning, instructional delivery, and assessment, but I still have a ways to go in classroom control."

"Sounds like you are doing as well as anyone would expect," Sandy Starr responded.

"The only thing I'm a bit confused about," said Nellie, "is exactly *how* I am to improve my classroom control. Mr. Rookie says not to let students take advantage of me or 'pull my chain,' as he calls it, but when I ask him for specifics, he says it's all about finding these secrets over time. Are the techniques for success really supposed to be discovered? If so, can you at least give me a hint?"

Sandy Starr responded, "We're all so busy, Nellie, Mr. Rookie included. Why don't you and I spend a bit of time after school tomorrow talking through some of these situations, as it appears we'll need to find another way of providing you the good advice that you need this time of year. I'll help you out, but let's keep this between us. With Judy as your mentor— well, allegedly, anyway—we wouldn't want to raise the ire of her group, would we?"

Sandy Starr thought to herself, *Maybe if Roger Rookie would spend a little less time placating those who care much less for children and much more for stipends, we would have a more effective induction and mentoring process around Anywhere Middle School. If I weren't so busy with standardized tests approaching, I would ask for a meeting with him myself, as I am a bit concerned he is being led around by the people who are not going to move our children forward.*

"Can I ask you another thing, Mrs. Starr?"

"Certainly, Nellie."

"Has Karl Chameleon been acting a bit different lately?

"Why do you ask?"

"Well, when I first took this job, he was always in his class next door with students having a good time. We would spend time between classes talking, and he even informed me of several students' names. Over the past few months, I haven't seen him as often, as he is spending much more time in the lounge."

"Nothing good is going to come of that," Sandy Starr said.

"I hear him yelling at students a bit more, which wasn't at all like him during the first part of this year. I'm just worried about him; that's all."

"Nellie, you have reason to be. He's not in good company."

Roger Rookie's Deep Thoughts

As Roger pondered more deeply his recent leadership style and its effects upon others and himself, a few things came to mind during some late-night reflection:

THE GLAD-HANDER'S EFFECTS ON STAFF...

SUPERSTARS

- Like it at first
- Get frustrated with unsolved problems
- Do NOT feel valued because all are treated the same

FENCESITTERS

- Love it!
- Do little work but feel entitled
- Their efforts go up at first, then diminish

BULLIES

- Continually become more demanding
- Milk the leader
- Have an underserved confidence level

THE GLAD-HANDER
CONTINUED...

THE LEADER FEELS
- Good for a very brief period
- That what he/she does is NEVER enough
- Taken advantage of

UNINTENDED CONSEQUENCES
- organization becomes unfocused
- over time, less work gets done
- The leader gains, then loses RESPECT

Chapter 4
Roger Rookie's Third Makeover: the Thumb

When Roger was a student teacher at Blue Collar Middle School, his principal was Ivan Ironside. Ironside, a former military captain with a shaved head that kept widening to the shoulders, was a no-nonsense principal.

As a student teacher, Roger had marveled at the tight ship he ran. Ironside seemed a bit intimidating and had complete control over every situation. Many of the problems facing Roger as a principal at AMS weren't present in Ironside's school. Roger gave Ironside all the credit. He couldn't imagine a teacher mouthing off to Ivan Ironside. Certainly, no one would dare stab him in the back—he might turn back around and clean their clock!

I need to talk with Mr. Ironside and get his advice on how to turn things around at Anywhere Middle School, Roger thought. He called Ironside's secretary to set up a meeting. *It will be nice to see things at Blue Collar again; it's been a while.*

As he parked his car at Blue Collar Middle School, he saw a custodian busily sweeping the front walk. Another was polishing the front handrails adjacent to the steps. In the distance, he saw a physical education class doing jumping jacks and push-ups. *Boy, it's cold weather, and these kids are outside! In my school, even the teachers would refuse to suit up for outside calisthenics.*

Before he could open the front door, a student hurried down from the office to open it, greeting him with: a "Welcome, sir, to Blue Collar Middle School, where we do more before 9 a.m. than most do all day!"

"Thank you, young man. I'm here to meet with Mr. Ironside."

"His office is right up the stairs, sir, just past our dress code checkpoint, next to the teachers' lesson-plan submission window. Have a nice day."

In the office, Roger spent a few moments catching up with a few of the secretaries who remembered him as a student teacher. One gave him a hug; another pinched his cheek. They couldn't believe he was all grown up—and a principal at that!

Roger took a seat alongside a few teachers who were waiting for Principal Ironside. One by one, each was quickly ushered into his office by the secretaries. Each teacher meeting lasted only a few moments before they emerged and walked briskly down the hallways, serious in gait, many with heads down, all tending to the business of "doing school."

What a machine! Roger marveled. *In quickly, out expediently, and all with a "Yes, sir, and can I have another?" look on their face. Now, this is leadership!*

"ROOKIE! I hear you're a principal now, young man! Any truth to that rumor?"

Roger stood quickly and snapped to attention with his arms at his side and feet together. In front of him, Ivan Ironside stood with the same marshal pose Roger remembered as he inspected the newbie from head to toe.

"At ease, Rookie; you're one of us now. How've you been, young man?"

"Very busy, Mr. Ironside. Thank you for taking time with me today."

When they sat down for coffee, Roger felt his heart rate increase. Ironside, although not intending to, still intimidated him.

"Rookie, my secretary tells me you're here for advice. If you and I were on a social visit, we'd go out into the woods and shoot things. Since that's not the case, there's no time to shoot anything, not even 'the bull.' Just give me the facts. The sooner I understand your theater of operation, the sooner we can deploy something."

"Yes, Mr. Ironside. It all began with . . ."

Roger told Ironside all about the course of events from the first faculty meeting to the launch of the school year. He told him about teachers complaining about Seminar, about their before-school duty, about the dysfunctional faculty meetings, and all the money he had spent on food.

"I have this group I call . . . "

Before Roger could say, "The Bullies" (and it was probably fortunate he did not), Ironside interrupted. "Stop! Rookie, who is running the show over there?! You need to man-*up* and start leading! I know you're still wet behind the ears, but good grief! Quit rolling belly-up for an abdominal scratch. People are walking all over you. You've been in my school; do you think I got my staff in tip-top shape by kissing everybody's backside all day?"

Roger shook his head and said, "But how do you keep the morale of the staff up?"

Ironside replied, "You want to know how to have good morale? Accomplish your mission! When I was a captain in the military, my soldiers had great morale when we implemented my plan and it was successful. When they didn't do things the right way, I chewed their butts. Are you hearing me, kid? You think your direct reports respect you? Based on what I am hearing, the answer is a big fat NO. Stop acting like a patsy. Start leading!"

Principal Ironside segued into stories of his early days in the service, where he honed and crafted his leadership under arduous conditions. Once stateside, he "took command" of his teaching staff the way he worked with recruits overseas.

"You have to be direct with your people," he concluded. "They work for *you*, not the other way around. Tell them what you want from them, command respect, and, above all, *accomplish your mission*. You're not there to make friends, and you're certainly not their darned bellhop. Stop pussyfooting around and put your *thumb* on those people!"

Roger thanked Ivan Ironside for meeting with him and giving him advice on how to fix the problems at AMS. On his way out the door, it was all Roger could do not to salute his former principal.

Back at Anywhere

A faculty meeting was scheduled for the following week, which gave Roger a few days to prepare. He had only one word on the faculty meeting agenda: CHANGE. In those few days, he reflected often on Ironside's advice, and each time, the stern words fueled his fire.

He scribbled a few thoughts onto his notepad:

ADVICE FROM
MR. IRONSIDE

1. YOU ARE NOT A PATSY...
START LEADING!

2. DON'T KISS PEOPLE'S
BACKSIDES!
(YUCK...
went
visual
on that
one) :(

3. BE DIRECT...
RESULTS WILL WIN
RESPECT!

(I think "this" is THE SECRET)

He installed a new mirror in his office, full length so that he could practice his new marshal pose. He bought a few new suits, charcoal (darker than what he typically would wear) with power ties in red, white, and blue. Shiny, black patent leather shoes with squared toes were a bit uncomfortable for him, but he was trying to get used to them.

Roger Rookie even hung a few pictures of leaders he now chose to admire, most of whom had won battles of one kind or another. He ordered a bigger chair for his desk. There were still three months left in the school year, and Roger Rookie was determined to use "real leadership" to improve Anywhere Middle School. The last thing he thought before he walked into the faculty meeting was, *MY way or the highway!*

The faculty meeting began promptly at 7:30.

"Welcome, ladies and gentlemen. Let's get right to the topic of changing this school, and make sure you take notes on what we'll be deploying. You'll have your marching orders shortly."

Teachers looked around at each other, a bit confused. A few thought Roger Rookie's new style was a bit cute as he tried it on for size.

"Did he spend the weekend watching General Patton movies?" Edgar whispered to Karl, pretending to slap him with a glove. Karl chuckled, but quickly stopped when Roger snapped a look in their direction.

LaVon Babble then walked in late, carrying a coffee and talking on her cell phone.

Roger Rookie looked directly at LaVon and said in a loud voice, "Mrs. Babble, you continue to arrive late for meetings and interrupt our work with your private conversation. It is rude and will not be tolerated. You need to leave."

LaVon Babble dropped her phone. The room was silent.

Roger Rookie pointed his finger at the door.

LaVon picked up her cell phone, looked at the Bullies who simply looked back at her, and then walked out of the room. Roger then turned to the staff with a click of his heel, prepared if anybody wanted to challenge his authority.

Mildred Morose stood up and began to speak. "Mr. Rookie, on behalf of the staff who just witnessed your handling of Mrs. Babble's arrival . . . "

Roger interrupted, "Mrs. Morose, you can sit down and be quiet or join Mrs. Babble. Your choice."

Roger's inside voice was incongruent with his outside demeanor.

What the heck are you doing, Roger, it said. *You're really out there on a limb, and you're liable to get it chopped off!* He was sure he might have a heart attack at any minute, but continued to glare at Mrs. Morose.

Mildred mumbled something the other Bullies heard and sat back down.

Roger returned to his agenda. Using the new pointer stick he had purchased from a military surplus store over the weekend, he paced back and forth in front of the portable screen set up for the meeting, tapping on the projected data from the standardized test scores the school had recently received.

He then stopped his march, turning "left face" to the staff and said, "The data is terrible! What do you think Central Office is going to think of this data?"

His staff just looked at him with deer-in-headlights expressions.

"Well guess what? Things are going to change around here."

"*All* staff will be held accountable for making AMS a premier school. It's going to start with doing your jobs! I don't want to hear if you *do* or *don't* like this or that, 'blah, blah, blah.'"

Roger marched back and forth at the front of the room. "If you don't like how prepared students are when they come to class, contact the parents yourselves! If you don't like some of the working conditions here at Anywhere, be thankful you have a place to work! If you don't like getting to meetings on time and paying attention, find someplace to work where you can show up late and read the newspaper! Most of all, remember that I'm your principal, not your concierge."

Roger spent the last ten minutes outlining what those changes entailed with respect to their curriculum, instruction, and student supervision. The meeting ended at 8:00 on the dot. Roger did not see any teachers checking papers, texting, or talking like he routinely saw during staff meetings.

He felt empowered.

It dawned on Roger as staff filed out of the room that not a single teacher spoke during the past half hour. Roger made a mental note to call Ivan Ironside and thank him for telling Roger how a leader behaves.

Student Issues

The morning's docket was to be filled with Roger dealing with student discipline. Coming off the faculty meeting victory, he decided to continue with his new leadership style. He noticed several students had been sent to the office—the same students as usual and from the same classrooms that always sent students to the office. Roger Rookie was sick of seeing the same students.

He decided it was time to treat students like he had just treated the staff. Roger called the first student into his office. "Why were you sent down here?" he asked.

"Well, Mr. Rookie, I simply left my homework in my locker, when I was kicked out for no reason."

"Last time I thought about a student's job description," said Roger, "it involved using the five minutes between classes to go to your locker, grab your materials for the next class, then proceed to that destination prepared for instruction. Am I correct?!"

"But Mr. Rookie . . . "

"No buts! Talking to you about leaving your homework in your locker is a waste of your parents' tax dollars! You should be in class doing *student* things, and I should be in my office doing *principal* things!! Talking about a part of your job description that a kindergartner could understand is embarrassing for both *you* and *me*. Have some pride. Get your act together!"

The student sat quietly until Mr. Rookie was done speaking.

"I'm giving you three nights of detention to teach you a lesson about your job description as a student. Off you go!!"

When Roger opened his office door, the other students waiting to see him looked at him with big eyes.

Roger met with the next student; however, unlike the first student, when Roger raised his voice, the student argued right back. As the conversation escalated and inappropriate comments were made, Roger suspended the student.

He suspended a boatload of students that day. And a boatload the next.

Roger decided he'd had enough with students getting sent to the office for stupid reasons. He sent the following email to the staff:

Faculty,

Over the past few months, I have noticed an increasing number of frivolous student referrals to my office, which have resulted in a loss of instructional time and decreased productivity for the office. Effective immediately, silly issues like forgotten pencils and homework left in lockers will be the responsibility of the teachers to correct. If students are sent to the office, it had better be for a good reason that is beyond the control of a professional faculty member to handle. In short, if you send a student to me, it will be an admission that you are unable to handle the situation, which may result in a meeting afterward for further training and corrective action on your behalf. If you have any problems with this new protocol, see me.

Educationally yours,

Mr. Rookie

On Patrol

On his rounds through the school later that week, Roger noticed Edgar Sleeper was not fulfilling his corridor supervision responsibility. Teachers were required to supervise the hallways between classes to keep students moving along and curtail inappropriate behavior. On his way past Edgar's classroom, Roger saw him sitting at his desk talking on his cell phone.

"Mr. Sleeper, why are you not on duty?"

Edgar quickly ended the phone call, saying, "Sorry, Mr. Rookie, important telephone call that needed my attention. I'll get right out in the hall."

"Electronic technology does not have a constitutional right to be answered during your professional working hours, Mr. Sleeper. Was there a death in the family?"

"No, Mr. Rookie, but . . . "

"Did someone lose a limb through amputation?"

"No, but . . . "

"Did you win the lottery, and thus will no longer have a need for employment at Anywhere?"

"No, but . . . "

"Then in my estimation, it was still your responsibility to supervise the hallway, and you were clearly not fulfilling your duty. You can expect a letter in your file noting the indiscretion."

Roger did a quick "about face," leaving Edgar speechless. Back in his office he fired off another school-wide email:

Faculty,

While on rounds today, I noticed faculty were not fulfilling their professional corridor supervision responsibilities as outlined in the performance expectations checklist provided to you at the outset of this school year. Faculty and staff found derelict of duty in the aforementioned will be handled according to the progressive and corrective disciplinary measures found in this year's Anywhere Middle School Faculty and Staff Handbook. I thank you for your anticipated cooperation.

Responsibly yours,

Mr. Rookie

Trudy Savage then appeared proudly at his door holding a stack of Post-It notes with the names and telephone numbers of angry parents. There were lots of notes.

"It's about time someone started making up for lost time, whipping these little heathens into shape," she said, scattering the notes across Roger's desk. "I took the liberty of telling these deadbeats, sir, that you'll call back when you're darned good and ready, and they'll rue the day they complained to Roger Rookie!"

"This looks like I'll be making calls long into the evening," Roger said.

"Nah, just tell them the way it's gonna be, and hang up. It's not rocket science!" Trudy added, "I'll leave the door ajar. Don't worry about keeping your voice down; it will help with deterrence."

She spun around, left his office, and barked at someone in the distance.

Roger got home very late that evening. Exhausted, he sat on the couch devouring popcorn, drinking his favorite soda, and watching late-night TV. He reflected on his newfound Ironside style.

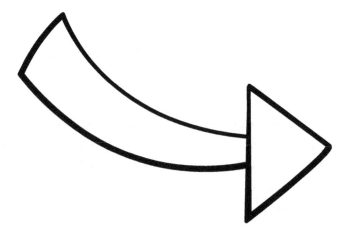

He had to admit, certain parts of this new, tough-guy attitude made the school day go very well. Apart from the initial interruptions he had nipped in the bud, the faculty meeting had gone smoothly. And he was confident office referrals would decrease. But there were other parts of the past few days he did not feel as good about. Yelling at students was not at all a fit for him, neither was arguing to the point that they used profanity and got themselves suspended. Roger decided he just needed to give the new style more time. People would adjust their behavior and actions once they got used to the new sheriff in town, Roger Rookie. *The law ain't for sale at Anywhere no more!*

The next day, Roger Rookie emailed LaVon Babble about meeting in his office.

Mrs. Babble,

Plan on arriving in my office within five minutes of tomorrow's closing bell to discuss the incident of your tardiness at our most recent staff meeting. Your tardiness at this meeting, if it occurs, will not reflect favorably on the outcome.

Promptly yours,

Mr. Rookie

LaVon Babble usually left school early to pick up her children, but she could sense she had better make other arrangements for her children and attend the meeting. After LaVon's short wait in the outer office where she felt like a student waiting to be disciplined, Roger Rookie opened his door and signaled for her to come in.

Roger Rookie looked directly at LaVon Babble, saying, "Mrs. Babble, as your principal I am directing you from this date forward to be on time and attentive for future faculty meetings; moreover, texting, checking papers, or talking while presentations are being made will be grounds for your removal from the meetings."

He then shared with LaVon Babble what was discussed at the meeting.

Roger closed the meeting by saying, "Mrs. Babble, you no longer have permission to leave early at the end of the day. If you cannot fulfill your contract, although my desk is full, I will find room on it for you to place your letter of resignation."

Roger Rookie then stood up and walked out of his office.

After a few seconds, LaVon Babble got up and left as well. Trudy Savage couldn't help but notice the tears on her face as she exited Roger Rookie's office. LaVon made a quiet phone call to the lounge, looking back over her shoulder.

In the front office lobby, Roger greeted Mr. and Mrs. Smith, parents of one of the school's seventh graders, and invited them back to his office. Closing the door, he asked the parents to state their concerns.

"Mr. Rookie, our daughter's grades are not at all acceptable; they have gone down each quarter. We would like to request help to get our daughter back on the right track."

"Mr. and Mrs. Smith, have teachers been in contact with you to keep you updated on your daughter's performance?

"Some of the teachers have been in contact with us," Mrs. Smith said. "But we have not heard at all from two teachers despite our continued attempts to share our email addresses, our work telephone numbers, and available times for meetings."

Roger immediately asked Trudy Savage to call the two teachers down to join them in the meeting.

He then stated, with the teachers present, that this neglect of duty was unacceptable, and he apologized to the parents for the teachers' lack of follow-up. He shared that he would follow up privately with the teachers and that the Smith family could expect frequent updates in the future. With their heads down, neither teacher said a word. The meeting concluded with the guidance counselor arranging for the parents and teachers to use a notebook journal for daily feedback and communication.

"Off you go!" said Roger Rookie to the two teachers. He then walked the Smiths to the school entrance and thanked them for their visit.

***

Karl Chameleon talked with students as Roger Rookie entered his room for pre-scheduled observation. As Karl began his lesson, he couldn't help but think of how much Roger had changed in recent weeks and how rudely he was treating teachers. The teachers' lounge had become a therapy room for teachers who had been bullied by "Robo-Rookie," as many now called Roger behind his back.

The staff had also noticed Roger sported a new haircut that made him look like a Marine recruit. Karl Chameleon stumbled through his lesson, feeling very uneasy with Roger's presence. He dreaded his post-observation conference, afraid of the criticism and potential attack. For the first time in a long time, Karl Chameleon thought about applying for a job at another school.

***

Nellie Newcomer arrived for a meeting in Roger Rookie's office. Roger had been so busy telling people what to do, he had not had the chance to meet with Nellie in several weeks. He requested she stop by and meet with him. Nellie stopped at the entry to Roger's office and waited for him to give her permission to enter.

"Come in, please, Miss Newcomer," Roger said.

After Nellie sat down, Roger began by saying, "Miss Newcomer, I continue to be impressed by your skills. Your lessons are creative, and students are always engaged when I observed your classroom. Further, you have one of the most organized classrooms at AMS. In less than a year, you have established yourself as a quality teacher." He paused and then asked, "How is the mentoring with Ms. Slacker going?"

"Mr. Rookie, nothing has changed since the last time we met. I can only count on one hand the number of times Ms. Slacker has met with me the entire year. I'm sorry to bring this up to you, but you have asked for my candor, and I respect your authority."

Mr. Rookie thanked Nellie for meeting with him, and as she left for her classroom, he immediately turned around and began typing an email. Roger had eight months of pent up frustration with Judy Slacker's horrible job of mentoring Nellie, and his frustration was coming out. He wrote a note to her, demanding a meeting for the next day, before school started.

Ms. Slacker,

It has come to my attention that you have continued to disregard my expectation that you provide mentoring to Miss Newcomer during her first year of teaching at Anywhere Middle School. I am thus directing you to a meeting in my office to be held thirty minutes prior to the start of school tomorrow morning. I trust you will be on time.

With concern and disappointment,

Principal Rookie

Judy Slacker arrived for school, walked quickly down to Roger Rookie's office, and found him sitting at his desk. As she entered his office, Roger said, "Ms. Slacker, will you please close the door."

Roger Rookie continued, "Ms. Slacker, you have failed miserably in your duties as Miss Newcomer's mentor. You have disregarded my admonitions to you with willful and wanton callousness to the needs of someone new to our profession. I am now beyond dismay at your professional performance. I am *angry!*"

Roger Rookie's shouting at Ms. Slacker could be heard in the outer office. He demanded that she begin meeting weekly with Nellie Newcomer. He warned her that he would be checking up on her, and if she did not obey his directions, there would be discipline for insubordination. She did not say a single word during the meeting.

Another Meeting, Thumb-Style

Roger Rookie was two months into his new style.

Students and staff seemed to have adjusted to how Roger wanted things done. Unlike earlier in the year when students and teachers came to Roger all the time, now almost nobody spoke with him. Although Roger missed talking to students, he did not miss always solving the teachers' problems. Yes, Roger felt like things were finally coming around at Anywhere Middle School.

Roger read through his agenda during the next faculty meeting. He hadn't bothered bringing food as he used to do. He had a lot of stuff to get through, so he skipped the Positive Comments item. He started by taking roll, a new practice Roger had implemented to make sure all staff members were in attendance and on time.

With a smile, he said, "I'm pleased that there is again perfect attendance today. We have some very important areas of focus I want to highlight, as we are nearing the end of our academic year. Now take note before I discuss these in detail: Even though there are only a few weeks of school left, AMS is *not* going to start playing games and watching movies. During my walk-throughs, I expect to see teachers teaching and students learning."

"Are there any questions?"

There were none.

Roger continued, "I also need to see more teachers supervising unstructured areas, specifically the hallways between classes. As you know, I've already had to reprimand a few of you for dereliction of duty."

A few heads went down with this comment. He was pleased that Mildred Morose did not make eye contact. What Roger Rookie failed to notice was that Sandy Starr and Nellie Newcomer didn't make eye contact with him either.

From the Bullies and a few others, looks of contempt were shot his way, but Roger did not pick up on these, as his focus was on his agenda.

Roger asked again, "Are there any questions?"

No questions.

"Alright, then! Let's remember our mission," Roger said, wrapping up the meeting. Not one teacher smiled or acknowledged their principal as they filed out of the room.

Thumbland Murmurs

Roger arrived early to school to finish some paperwork before his morning patrol. As he made his rounds, he heard his name mentioned.

Roger slowed down and eavesdropped on the conversation. He couldn't wait to crack down on this group of malcontents who were most likely poisoning his school.

As Mr. Rookie continued to listen, however, he realized the voice was Sandy Starr's, one of his best teachers.

Mrs. Starr continued, "I am very uncomfortable with anybody in the building, students or staff members, being treated disrespectfully. Mr. Sleeper shared with me that he was talking on his cell phone with his mother who is battling cancer, and when he missed a hall duty, Mr. Rookie wrote a letter of reprimand and placed it in his file. He didn't even give Mr. Sleeper a chance to explain why he was on the telephone."

Nellie Newcomer added, "He yelled at Ms. Slacker and ordered her to meet with me every week. Now she treats me worse than ever. I hate meeting with her, but I have to, or she will be in trouble. I probably will also. It's like having detention. I just sit there with her. She doesn't say anything to me, and I cannot get any work done."

Roger realized it was time for him to quit listening to a conversation that clearly was not intended for his ears. Dejected, he slowly walked to his office.

Teachers' Lounge

"Hey, you hear how many principals it takes to get through the year at Anywhere Middle School?" said Karl Chameleon, a little softer than usual, as sometimes lounge conversations could be heard from the hallway.

"C'mon Chameleon, give it a rest!" someone said.

"*Two*: one to start off as Dr. Jekyll, and the next to make Mr. Hyde seem more like Mr. Rogers!"

Groans and a chuckle or two floated around the room.

"That's stupid, Karl, but fairly accurate," someone retorted.

"It's certainly not a wonderful day in this neighborhood for any of us, is it?" Mildred Morose said.

"Certainly not for me," said LaVon Babble. "I'm now struggling to arrange my family's schedule after school; it's taking a toll on all of us."

"Nellie Newcomer and I are now forced to meet each week," said Judy Slacker." That girl didn't need my help in the first place. I don't know what to say to her. It's awkward. She's doing just fine, as we all know. And Robo-Rookie's now got her afraid that if she and I miss a meeting, she'll be in his office getting verbally abused, as I was."

"We should probably invite her down here every once in a while to get her out of the crosshairs," Karl Chameleon chimed. "Although you all are a bit hard to digest sometimes, we're not the monsters Rookie makes us out to be."

That comment was met with a few giggles.

"Now, I resemble that remark," Mildred said. "I wear my recalcitrance with a badge of honor. Just call me Queen B, and we all know 'B' doesn't stand for 'badge'!"

"Hey, what are y'all doing over the summer?" Karl Chameleon asked.

"Getting as far away from here as possible!" Edgar Sleeper snorted.

"Amen to that, brother!" said Karl.

"In the old days, I would actually do a bit of summer school. Liked the extra cash, but if you think I'm going to be worried about hallway duty and write-ups for a few extra thousand dollars, think again. I'd rather go out and do something else without having to worry about Robo's wrath and a weekly visit to his whipping post."

The lounge door opened, and with a sheepish look on her face, in walked Nellie Newcomer.

"Hey, look who it is," Mildred Morose said. "Sweet Polly Purebred herself."

"Hi, everyone. I don't mean to disturb you all. Would you mind if I microwaved my Lean Cuisine? Mrs. Savage has moved the front office microwave to the bookroom behind her desk, and I'm not allowed in there. I wouldn't want to disturb Mr. Rookie with something such as this."

"Better than that," Mildred said. "Nuke that thing, then why don't you have a seat with us and enjoy your lunch. We were just talking about you. Don't worry, we won't bite."

"Congrats on your first year, Nellie," said Edgar Sleeper.

"Made it through the gauntlet," said Karl Chameleon.

"She's a good kid," said Judy Sleeper.

Although Nellie thought Judy to be a bit insincere, she did feel good with the well wishes.

This was a group that intimidated her a bit, but they always seemed to enjoy themselves. Maybe if she spent a bit more time with them, she could earn their respect and keep a great professional friendship with Mrs. Starr.

Nellie Newcomer liked the camaraderie, but felt odd and guilty for visiting the lounge. Her feelings confused her, but for the first time, she felt welcomed by the Teachers' Lounge group.

The Coffee Klatch

Nellie must be tied up today more than usual, thought Sandy Starr. *I can understand that. The end of a first year is quite trying. I'm so very proud of her.*

Most of the coffee klatch's regulars had left the weekly meeting a bit early. Everyone seemed to be worried about getting their grades submitted in a timely fashion. "Mr. Rookie's got Trudy Savage on 'final grade watch,'" she'd been told. No one wanted to risk incurring the wrath of either Robo-Rookie or Mrs. Savage.

Sandy Starr opened her laptop and read an email from the district superintendent announcing the retirements that were to take place as well as the dates for upcoming congratulatory receptions for those employees.

I must be sure to make a few of these receptions, she thought. As she scanned the list of retiring teachers, she saw an opening in her content area in another middle school. *Gosh! Over the years, I would have never thought that I wanted to be anywhere else but Anywhere.* Now, with the ongoing negativity of staff, coupled with Roger's newfound and disrespectful totalitarianism, she no longer felt that loyalty to AMS. *I wonder if I shouldn't use my seniority to make a change. Maybe I'll talk to my husband over dinner tonight.*

With that, Sandy Starr began studying the staff roster for the district's other middle school and smiled when she saw a few names she recognized.

Principal's Evaluation

Roger twiddled his thumbs and doodled nervously while awaiting his end-of-year evaluation with Mr. Superintendent. He clearly remembered his boss's charge at the beginning of the year: "What I need you to do immediately in Anywhere Middle School, Rookie, is to change the focus from that of teachers and teaching to that of learning. I want results, not just forming a committee. I want that place turned around."

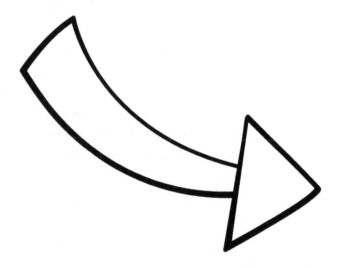

Hmmm...

Are we about

"TEACHERS," (don't think so)

"TEACHING," (maybe)

"CLIMATE," (can't hurt)

"ACCOUNTABILITY,"
(gotta have some)

And HOW DOES THIS
RESULT IN

LEARNING?
(still confused, a bit)

The superintendent's voice echoed in Roger's mind as he asked himself, *Am I on track?* Standardized test scores were scheduled to arrive over the summer, and more than anything else, Roger wanted another crack at a reinvention of Anywhere. *There's always that natural do-over when the new school year arrives,* he anticipated. *I can't wait to see what we can accomplish, now that I'm settling into doing some real leading with those folks.*

"Roger, can I get you anything to drink while the superintendent finishes with his telephone calls?"

Cindy Sage was always a gracious host for those visiting Central Office.

Roger always valued the time he spent in her office. Though he nervously anticipated the visit with his boss, the atmosphere of the outer office reminded him a bit of his mom's living room at home. He felt Mrs. Sage was on his side.

"Thank you for that, Mrs. Sage. Yes, I would love some coffee, if it isn't too much trouble."

"Of course not, Roger. Grab that mug right over there; I'll pour."

"Thank you."

"I hear things have been changing at Anywhere, Roger. You're moving forward with a new leadership style, from what I understand."

Roger, a bit taken aback, wondered how she had heard about this. "You've heard that, huh?" he asked.

"Why, yes, Roger. It is the talk of the district."

"I owe a good deal of credit to Mr. Ironside from Blue Collar Middle School," said Roger. "Much as his teachers did for me when I was student teaching in his school, he has encouraged me to dig deep into my leadership style. I think it has helped move our school forward, as my boss expects."

"How is the new style working for you, Roger. Does it fit you as well as it does Ivan Ironside?"

Roger answered by not answering. Skirting the question, he told Mrs. Sage many of the things that had happened over the previous ten weeks. He did his best to shine the most positive light on the increased accountability teachers and students felt with respect to their roles in the school. He shared other positive outcomes, saying, "I have had more productive faculty meetings, staff are doing what I am asking, and the Bullies have quit complaining."

Mrs. Sage then asked, "Have you sought out the advice of any of your superstar teachers on this change of leadership style? It would be very interesting to get their feedback as you set some leadership goals for next year, don't you think?"

Roger thought to himself, *Well . . . not really; in fact, in the past three months, I cannot even recall more than two occasions in which I have spoken with Sandy Starr. Even my talks with Nellie Newcomer have been more focused on whether she and Judy Slacker have met, as opposed to her progress and success.*

Not one pat on the back, not one expression of gratitude, and not even one invitation to a faculty social or even a graduating senior's open house. I always thought principals and staffs were supposed do these sorts of things as years ended and summers approached. Gosh! I have been too busy to even miss that I'm not being included in anything that I'm not demanding others to do.

"Roger . . . Roger . . . are you still with me? You look lost in thought."

"Oh, it's nothing, Mrs. Sage. Maybe it's just that I'm a bit nervous for my end-of-year evaluation. I guess we're all nervous when we're being held accountable, aren't we?"

Mrs. Sage shared, "Accountability is critical for any organization to function at a high level, and a school without accountability will never be able to help every student reach his or her potential. A leader without accountability will never grow as a leader. It says much for you to embrace this, Roger.

"I do want to ask you a question, though. Do you think emulating Ivan Ironside's style of leadership has allowed others to get to know more of you as the leader operating from your core beliefs, or is it causing dissonance between who you are and whom you feel you need to be to accomplish your goals?"

Roger thought for a moment and said, "To be quite frank, Mrs. Sage, I'm not sure. My staff follows my orders, and students are more compliant, but I'm not sure I am leading how I thought I would when I graduated from principal school."

"That may very well be okay," Mrs. Sage responded reassuringly. "We all are finding our way as best we can. We all are doing the best we know how in school each day, aren't we? That includes our students, faculty, and staff, Roger. We all are just people taking our lives one day at a time."

Why Roger's thoughts flashed instantly to LaVon Babble juggling her schedule with her family's needs, he didn't know. He tried to block out that thought. He had too much on his mind to worry about how she managed her personal time.

"Roger, think of a great leader you know, or one you have known at some point in your life."

Roger searched his memory. "That would be Mr. Good, my middle school teacher and coach."

"Why was he great, Roger?"

"Well, he had high expectations. He had the ability to develop personal relationships with all of us while at the same time challenging us to improve performance. When we had individual needs requiring extra consideration, such as family problems or hardships, he would work things out as best he could to make reasonable accommodations for us. And he believed in us."

"Roger, great leaders like Mr. Good understand that fundamental to people reaching their potential, they have to be held accountable—something that is not always met with appreciation in the heat of the moment. On the other hand, great leaders also offer something to counterbalance this accountability, a climate that makes folks want to perform in ways they typically wouldn't without positive relationships."

"You know, Mrs. Sage, that makes sense," Roger said with a smile. "Anybody who has been fortunate enough to have a special teacher, coach, mentor, or boss who brought out the best in them had moments during the relationship where they were upset with the constant feedback on how to improve."

Roger's mind wandered again: *Great leaders demand excellence. And when somebody is not performing to his or her potential, the **great leader** continues to communicate why the performance level needs to improve and how they are going to work together for the improvement. But what sets a leader apart from an* *authoritative "boss" is that great leaders bring out the best in people and, at the same time, engage in a relationship built on trust and respect.*

Mrs. Sage spoke again. "It's not uncommon, Roger, for people to take weeks, months, or even years to appreciate how a great leader helped them perform at levels they did not fully appreciate at the time. Give yourself a pat on the back for doing what you could this past year, as best as you could. After all, didn't you, as did your staff, come to school each day and do the best you knew how?"

Suddenly, Roger experienced a "light bulb" moment.

He had been an *either/or* leader trying desperately to address the demands of a *both/and* school. Like a pendulum, his leadership had swung wildly from climate to accountability as he desperately tried to improve a focus on learning. Neither leadership style on its own had done the job in creating a learning-centered environment.

In thinking of the leadership of Mr. Good and others who'd had a powerful impact on his life, he knew he couldn't expect performance to improve with "either/or." He couldn't do pendulum-style leadership. He certainly couldn't continue putting his thumb on his superstar teachers who instead needed to be liberated and emulated. Only a "both/and" approach would move things where they needed to go.

Feeling liberated himself, Roger smiled at Mrs. Sage and said, "I'm feeling a lot better about my evaluation today. Thank you."

After his meeting with his superintendent, he hurried home and sketched out some of his revelations.

Roger Rookie's Deep Thoughts

As Roger pondered more deeply his recent leadership style and its effects upon others and himself, a few things came to mind in some late-night reflection.

THE THUMB'S EFFECTS ON STAFF...

SUPERSTARS
- Feel restricted/stop taking risks
- Cut themselves off from the rest of the school
- Are upset when their colleagues are disrespected

FENCESITTERS
- Align with bullies for protection
- Become overcome with inaction
- Never take a risk

BULLIES
- Move from obvious to subversive
- Provide refuge for others
- Lie in the weeds, waiting to strike!

THE THUMB
CONTINUED...

THE LEADER FEELS
- Empowered at first
- Sad, when he/she realizes
  the positive people are afraid
  and avoid him/her

- completely alone

UNINTENDED CONSEQUENCES
- Good people either side with the bad
  or want to leave the school
- Everyone works against the leader,
  or at minimum...wait for mistakes
- Leader loses support of students,
  parents, staff, and community

That's when it happened! Roger Rookie saw something vividly in his mind's eye that he knew he needed to draw before it left him. The secret was revealing itself in a way that wasn't even that secretive. Things were now making sense. He sketched his new understanding in his notebook.

Interlude
Summer Sunshine

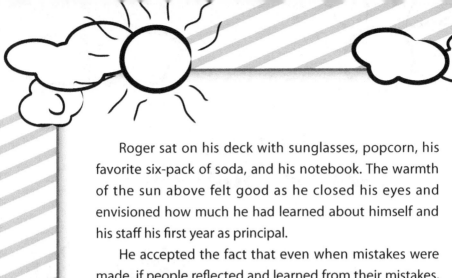

Roger sat on his deck with sunglasses, popcorn, his favorite six-pack of soda, and his notebook. The warmth of the sun above felt good as he closed his eyes and envisioned how much he had learned about himself and his staff his first year as principal.

He accepted the fact that even when mistakes were made, if people reflected and learned from their mistakes, it was growth. Instead of beating himself up, Roger decided to chalk up his first year in administration as a learning experience and vowed not to make the same mistakes again.

The first thing he did was read.

Not just more "how to be a principal" books.

Roger made a list of his heroes, past and present . . . those in education and outside education. He made lists of what qualities, attributes, and deeds caused them to be held in such high regard. Then he read biographies on them all! Not just autobiographies, those that put a spin on life accomplishments . . . but real biographies, the kind that share leaders' good points and bad, their heroic deeds and blemishes. He wanted to learn about real leading from real stories of the giants he hoped to stand on the shoulders of someday.

Roger also reached out for help and support. He called on other principals, respected teachers, and coaches and asked them how they handled different situations. He drew T-charts and made lists, so that he could learn

all he could learn all he could about a healthy balance between accountability and climate.

At times, Roger received completely different responses from leaders. That was okay, as he never reacted or judged the person. He was interested in hearing why leaders chose a particular method or strategy, thinking again, as Cindy Sage had mentioned, "We are all bringing the best we know how to school each day, aren't we?"

Roger even had lunch with Joel Gerrymander on one occasion and Ivan Ironside on another, to thank them for helping him find his way. By August, Roger knew what had to be done at Anywhere Middle School. He was excited and ready to continue to strive for a great school culture with a both/and approach of celebrating a positive climate while holding people accountable, starting with himself.

Chapter 5
Roger Rookie's Final Makeover: The Pathfinder

Roger was ready for his second year as principal. As he walked into his back-to-school faculty meeting, his last thought was, *Together, we will make a difference.* He realized, *I don't have to prove who is in charge; everybody knows who is in charge. And the more I try to prove it, the more everybody tries to prove me wrong.*

"Welcome back, everyone," Roger Rookie said. "After we meet our new faculty and staff, let's all share some of the great things we experienced this past summer."

Most folks were a bit gun-shy.

Fearful of Roger's reaction to what they might share, they didn't share much. After all, he had ended the previous year as "The Thumb." Roger sensed their apprehension and didn't want to pretend it was invisible to him.

"I want to say I feel a bit of the uneasiness in the room. I understand. You're wondering, first of all, why I'm smiling so much today, and probably—legitimately—when I'll wipe that smile off my face and begin cracking the whip."

Pocketed murmurs confirmed his perception.

"What I would like you to know about Roger Rookie as we begin this school year is this: As your principal, I very much appreciate all the guidance and support you provided me in my first year." (It was a true comment for most of his faculty and staff.) "My first year as a principal was much like my first year as a teacher. It had rewarding moments that validated my decision to be an educator. And there were a few moments when I left school and wondered why I didn't join the circus."

A few people chuckled.

"Or 'the military,' you're probably thinking," Roger added.

A smattering of nervous laughter was heard throughout the room as people began to loosen up just bit.

Roger continued, "I love what I do, at least on most days. I always strive to get better. It took me a few years as a teacher, but eventually I was told I did a pretty good job. I pledge to you that I will bring that same attitude to the principal position. We have a great team here at AMS, and I am really excited for our new school year. Please give me the time to show you how I have grown this past summer in reflection of my abilities as a leader, in consideration of the fine job you all do in leading your classrooms. Welcome all, to a new beginning!"

Staff members looked around at each other, still uncomfortable, not saying much. They turned their attention back to Roger Rookie.

The first business item on the agenda was to announce the building leadership team. Over the summer, Roger had contacted a group of teachers whom he knew were the most effective teachers at AMS. He had asked each of them to join the leadership team. Not surprisingly, many of the teachers were leery of accepting, especially Sandy Starr. Roger had persisted, explaining to the teachers that he would support them. He knew the school could only go as far as they took it—together. Eventually, he was able to convince all the most effective teachers to be on the leadership team.

"Chairing that team will be Mrs. Sandy Starr," Roger announced with a smile.

The response to the announcement was immediate. Mildred Morose asked, "Mr. Rookie, how exactly was the leadership team formed?"

"Mrs. Morose, I personally contacted teachers to serve on the committee based on the qualities and attributes I felt they had that could contribute to the mission of the committee's charge."

LaVon Babble inquired quickly, "Other teachers will also serve on the committee, won't they?"

Roger casually responded, "I appreciate the interest; however, the leadership committee is full this year, but I do know there are other committees that could benefit from your service, Mrs. Babble. Might you be interested in the holiday party planning committee?"

Several staff members were not sure what had just happened.

Roger continued down the agenda.

Edgar Sleeper said, "But Mr. Rookie . . ."

Roger quickly and respectfully said, "No worries, Mr. Sleeper, I'll put you down for the holiday committee as well. Please feel free to see me privately after the meeting if you wish to discuss anything further."

When Roger got to "teacher duties," he paused and reminded himself to be strong.

Roger announced, "Because of the instructional needs of our students, the school will revert back to five more minutes of Seminar time and teachers will be supervising the commons area before school."

A frenzy of talking began.

Finally, Mildred Morose said in a loud voice, "Why in the world should we get cheated out of five minutes of lunch and have to supervise the commons when we should be preparing for class?! Last year was the best year I've had in my thirty-year career, and I have no intention of doing a duty that is not asked of high school teachers. If you try to implement these changes, you can expect a grievance!"

Roger looked around the now-silent room. Very few eyes were able to muster the courage to look at him. Mildred even sat back down.

He said, "Having the paraprofessionals cover lunch and the commons duty last year was a mistake. I take full responsibility. I did it to help teachers because I know you have demanding jobs; however, that decision was not in the best interest of our students or that of the paraprofessionals."

Sandy Starr smiled, giving a nod to Nellie Newcomer.

"We have a great faculty that has the training and experience to help our students in academic situations. We cannot and will not give that duty to other hard-working staff members simply because we do not want to do it."

Sandy Starr raised her hand to speak.

"Yes, Mrs. Starr?"

"I never thought having our paraprofessionals cover our duties was the right thing for our students or our school. Even though I, too, enjoyed the additional time spent in planning, we need to ensure we are the ones instructionally and behaviorally supervising our students."

A few nodded.

Sandy Starr continued, "Last year I noticed an increase in students complaining about name calling and harassment before school, so I think we'll need to be vigilant from the first day to restore order and be clear about our expectations before school and during lunch."

Roger Rookie could not have said it better.

Later in the meeting, as Roger discussed the changes in how data would be analyzed, he noticed the Bullies were talking with each other. As he paused, the Bullies continued to talk loudly and draw attention. Roger even heard his name mentioned.

As Roger looked around the room, it was obvious to him the rest of the staff was not comfortable with what was happening. Knowing he had to strike a balance of dealing with the issue and still treating everybody with respect, he kept his composure and walked over to the area of the room where the Bullies sat. He looked directly at Mildred Morose and said, "Ladies and gentlemen, may we please have attention at our meeting? We have many important items to discuss, and I value your time in allowing the agenda to continue."

Mildred Morose made a snide remark, and rather than taking the bait, he thanked them for showing him the same respect he knew they demanded from their students.

He then walked back to the front of the room and made his next big announcement—one he knew would be very unpopular with some staff. He said, "The leadership team and I have discussed the achievement gaps between those students with special needs and those without. Beginning this school year, most special education students will receive their reading and math instruction in the regular education classrooms. Staff will utilize a co-teaching model when appropriate for the students."

The response came exactly as he expected.

One teacher said, "Do you realize the effect the inclusion model will have on the rest of the students?! What about the effect on the teachers? I don't want those kids in my classroom!"

Another said, "I have concerns trying to co-teach with other teachers in the building."

Roger allowed the faculty to share their concerns. When all the objections had been raised, he acknowledged the teachers' concerns and affirmed it would be a learning process for all. "We must ensure every decision we make has the best interests of our students at its foundation rather than the goal of preserving a traditional structure and delivery of teaching," Roger said.

He finished discussion by saying, "Please trust in these major decisions that significant professional development time will be made available during the year for all of us to plan and problem solve on how best to implement the new service model. Other support agencies will help us implement the co-teaching model that has had impressive, positive results in schools across the country."

On a roll now, he announced more changes that were coming to AMS.

Roger told the staff that the two new teachers, Nathan Neophyte and Sally Sterling would both need mentors. "Starting immediately, mentorships will be posted, and interested teachers can apply. I will then select mentors I think will provide the best support for the needs of the teachers."

Most of teachers took this in stride; Judy Slacker snorted.

The rest of the meeting was relatively uneventful. When it was over, Roger walked to his office with a sigh of relief and a little bounce to his step.

Unfinished Business

Later in the day, Roger was dropping off a note in a teacher's mailbox when he heard Trudy Savage say, "Well, I knew you would finally have to show your chubby-cheeked little face in the office."

He looked around the corner to see Sally Sterling standing in the front office with a nervous look on her face, cheeks admittedly chubby and a bit flushed at that greeting. Roger had hired Sally over the summer. She reminded him quite a bit of Nellie Newcomer. He was convinced she was going to be a great teacher for AMS.

Unaware of his presence, Trudy Savage blared, "Who do you think you are to come into this school and start taking items that do not belong to you?" Sally Sterling lowered her head and did not dare speak.

Roger spoke up, "Mrs. Savage, what is your concern?"

Trudy Savage looked at Roger Rookie dismissively and then stated as accusatorily as possible, "This girl apparently was raised to think it's okay to take items that do not belong to her. Without asking, she has taken the extra printer we had in the teacher's work room."

The office was full of staff members going about their business, but they had all gone quiet at Trudy's berating of Miss Sterling. All eyes were now on Roger Rookie.

Roger said to Sally Sterling, "I am so sorry for this confusion. I told you to take the extra printer for your room; you have done nothing wrong."

Roger then looked at Trudy Savage and said, "Mrs. Savage, will you please accompany me to my office?"

There was no mistaking the seriousness in Roger Rookie's tone or the look on his face.

Trudy Savage responded, "You will have to wait, as I have several important things I must get done for the children of this community, prior to their arrival."

Teachers watched with shock and awe.

Roger firmly, but without raising his voice, said, "We will meet in my office in thirty minutes, and you are advised to bring a union representative with you."

Trudy Savage muttered, "I guess the children and everyone else will just have to wait, so that your needs can be met, Mr. Principal!"

She left the office to call a union representative.

A Closed-Door Meeting

Roger began the meeting by saying, "Mrs. Savage, what happened with Miss Sterling will never happen again."

"Won't have to, Mr. Rookie, if you would stop giving printers to all the young women on staff. Must be nice to have friends with benefits."

Roger maintained his composure and continued. "Aside from your consistent unprofessionalism, Mrs. Savage, your interpersonal skills with students, staff, and community members have been unsatisfactory and must improve immediately. I will begin drafting an improvement plan that will be very specific on the areas of concern and the specific actions you must take to be successful."

With that, Trudy Savage pointed her finger at Roger and told him that she loved the students who deserved such, and further, had earned the respect of the staff. "The *only* parents who do not appreciate the way I conduct myself are the no-good, irresponsible parents who do not deserve to be treated with kindness. And, I might add, they should have practiced better birth control."

What on earth has created this angry, foul disposition in this person?! Roger thought to himself. *It's just unbelievable!*

Trudy Savage finished her verbal onslaught by jabbing a finger in Roger's chest, stating, "I have been at Anywhere Middle School long before your arrival and will be here long after you are gone."

Roger counted to ten before he spoke, wanting to let the intensity of Trudy's actions diminish. He couldn't believe what had just happened. He'd gotten thumped in the chest by one of his employees.

"Mrs. Savage," he said calmly, "You are being suspended from work for, in part, conduct unbecoming an educator. You will be put on paid administrative leave pending an investigation and deliberation for potential further discipline. Further, you are to submit to me your keys and leave immediately. Any further misconduct will lead to additional discipline."

For the first time in her career, Trudy Savage had no response.

Roger wanted to be sure his terms were crystal clear. "You are not permitted on school property until further notice," he said. "Someone from Central Office will be contacting you within three days, and you will be given due process during the handling of these incidents. I will walk you to the exit."

Trudy Savage began to speak, but thought better of it.

She threw her keys on Roger's desk and defiantly stormed out of her office.

Roger stayed a few feet behind, but escorted her to her car.

Several teachers were in the office and tried to look busy while watching their principal escort Mrs. Savage out of the building. "It's about time Trudy Savage walked her own Green Mile," someone said. Word about the secretary's dismissal spread like wildfire.

After Trudy Savage had driven away, Roger Rookie returned to the building and went immediately to Sally Sterling's room to apologize again for Trudy's behavior and to make sure she was okay.

At the end of the day, Roger returned to his office and noticed his voice message light on his phone was blinking. The message was from the associate superintendent who said, "Roger, I would like to inform you that a Mrs. Mildred Morose from your school contacted me complaining about your taking time from their lunch and implementing a special education system without any staff input or support. I want to assure you, Roger, that after reviewing our policies and agreements we have in place, I am not concerned with the complaint. I just wanted you to be aware that a call came from your building. Please know that I have complete confidence in you. It's about time somebody started holding the AMS adults to task. Have a great start to the school year."

Roger smiled and played the message a second time.

Out and About

The next day, Roger visited Nellie Newcomer's room first thing in the morning. He handed her a large cup of her favorite drink, chai tea.

Nellie smiled, "Thank you, Mr. Rookie."

Roger began, "I am here today to apologize to you. Last year was your first year, and I did a poor job of providing you with the support you needed and deserved. I am determined to make things right this year. Although it is your second year, and you are on my leadership team, which indicates my level of respect for you, I have asked Mrs. Starr to serve officially as your mentor this year. You are a very good teacher, Nellie, and with a little bit of coaching, you will be a great teacher. I predict you will be serving as a mentor in a few years."

"Thank you so much, Mr. Rookie. I want you to know, as well, that I went home really excited yesterday," Nellie said. "I could tell from how you led the faculty meeting that this is going to be a special year at AMS."

Roger smiled. "Nellie, I'll be checking in frequently to see what else I can provide for you. Thanks for all you do."

Roger then walked around the school and watched the teachers as they worked frantically to complete last-minute details for the first day of school. As Roger walked into Karl Chameleon's classroom, he said, "Karl, tell me more about your trip you mentioned briefly at staff meeting."

"Went to Yellowstone, saw the sights, did all the fun stuff. Took in a geyser! It is definitely a special end of the world out there," Karl said. He talked about his trip for a good ten minutes. When he had finished, Roger gestured around the room and said, "What's all this, Karl? Your classroom really looks different!"

Roger Rookie noticed Karl Chameleon had actually decorated his classroom. Last year, Karl's room was pretty bland; this year, it had been given a major makeover.

Karl responded, "After our last summer leadership meeting, I asked Mrs. Starr about her room, and she gave me several great ideas on surrounding students with motivation that included student work. I have to say, I think my room looks a lot better."

"Sure does, Karl. It looks *great!*"

"I was also very excited last summer, Karl, when you accepted the offer to be on our leadership team. Folks really like you, Karl, and your ideas are top-notch! We just need to give you more opportunities to share them with people who will add value to the conversation and help make them a reality. I think our team will do just that."

Building Leadership Team Meeting

In early September, the building leadership team met for its monthly meeting, reviewing several of the changes Roger Rookie had communicated at the faculty meeting at the beginning of the year. When the agenda shifted to new items, Sandy Starr brought up the reading series that had unanimous support from the leadership team, the same series Roger had ignored last year.

Roger looked around the room and said, "First, we have to review the curriculum. Which team members would be willing to meet and go over the curriculum with me?"

Sandy enthusiastically raised her hand, as did a couple other members of the leadership team.

"Fantastic!"

Roger continued, "It will challenge our budget, but if this group thinks the new curriculum is a good idea, I will do everything possible to make it happen. I sincerely value and appreciate your focus on learning."

Roger then asked, "Do you still feel that the professional development we discussed during the summer—with its focus on the new special education delivery plan—is where we should concentrate our efforts and expenditures?"

"Absolutely, Mr. Rookie," Nellie Newcomer said.

"Sure thing," Karl Chameleon added.

"I agree," Sandy Starr affirmed.

Unanimous in their belief that it was critical to provide significant support and resources for staff in a new model of instruction, they spent the remainder of the meeting planning ways to help the staff through the transition. Unlike his building leadership team meetings last year, this group of mission-mindful professionals reenergized Roger and helped him focus on the important things.

New Business as Usual

Roger could not believe two months of school had already passed. He felt that one of the biggest mistakes he had made in his first year as principal was the decision to "get tough" with students, as it had a negative on his relationship with students and parents. Frankly, it stymied communication. His new approach for students in disciplinary situations was to focus not only on accountability for their actions, but also on the climate of the conversation. He wanted them to learn about responsibility, and he wanted to give students an opportunity to speak for and think through things themselves. With those goals in mind, he asked them a series of questions so they could reflect on their actions and/or behaviors, which almost always led to students figuring out what they needed to do in the future to avoid making poor choices. This made for much better school, family, and community partnerships. It wasn't lost on him that this approach was very similar to the conversations he'd had with Cindy Sage at Central Office.

Roger used a similar approach when addressing staff behavior. And this year, when one or two staff members were doing something unsatisfactory like showing up late for work, Roger now *never* communicated the problem as though everybody was doing something wrong. He realized his former method of attempting to correct staff behavior by sending school-wide emails or making announcements about a problem made his most effective teachers feel uncomfortable because they immediately remembered the one time in their entire careers they had shown up late. Conversely, the employees who showed up late frequently disregarded the mass communication and actually found protective cover in it, thinking to themselves, *Hah! I must not be the only one.*

In just a short time, Roger had a handful of "opportunities" to put his new individualized problem-solving feedback into practice. In one instance, he met privately with a teacher who was consistently late with deadlines and offered clear expectations and a workable plan for accomplishing them. In another, he shared with staff members how people were reacting to his consistent negativity in monthly meetings. These were only two examples of how Roger was addressing concerns at their source, and in each instance, he was focusing on the behavior, not the person. And he used "I" messages to share how he felt about what was going on. This allowed him to maintain the dignity for all involved and focus on the issue that could be changed, while offering respect and positive regard for the person who needed to improve professional performance.

Balancing Climate with Accountability

During a late-fall workshop, Roger met with all teachers who were scheduled for professional performance evaluations that year. Many of the teachers knew it was "their year," and Roger Rookie had wanted to give them a bit of time to get things off the ground. Two teachers, however, were surprised to learn they were being evaluated. Roger agreed to meet with each individually to explain why this had occurred, informing them that "every three years" was the "minimum" for evaluation, by contract. He had the authority to schedule more, if needed.

Roger said to each, "Because I believe that, as your instructional leader, I can provide the support and supervision to help you improve in key areas, a formal evaluation process is the appropriate method to address the areas of concern. It keeps us all on the same page, and that page focuses on student learning."

One of the teachers to be evaluated this year was Mildred Morose. After a few minutes of small talk, he began the post-observation meeting by asking, "Mrs. Morose, what are your thoughts on the lesson?"

Mildred replied, "Well, of course it was a good lesson, given the students I have to work with this year, Roger."

Roger probed deeper, "What exactly do you mean, Mrs. Morose?"

Her trademark frown appeared, "Isn't it obvious we have a disadvantage at AMS? Our students don't come to school prepared, and I can tell you why, as I had most of their parents in school, and they were no picnic either. Guess what? The apples did not fall far from the trees. It's basic biology, really."

Roger Rookie's Final Makeover: The Pathfinder

Roger shook his head in disbelief. "Mrs. Morose, you have the same students as all the other teachers here at AMS, yet your student achievement data is consistently lower than your colleagues. You contend that students are the variable, but I believe you own some of this responsibility as the teacher as well."

He continued, "A good teacher finds a way to help all students learn. Mrs. Morose, I am going to draft an improvement plan with you and provide you with the necessary support and resources to improve your teaching. If you are willing to change your instructional practices, I know you can be a quality teacher; however, it is going to require you to do things differently."

Her face flushed with anger as she spoke, "Rookie, if I knew this meeting was going to include you threatening to fire me, I would have brought my union representative. What you are doing is illegal, and I can probably get you fired."

Roger did not respond. He simply got up, walked toward the door, turned to Mildred Morose and said, "I'll begin drafting the improvement plan. Oh, and yes, as a courtesy to you, I will remember to include your union representative when I schedule our next meeting." With that, he left the room.

Later that day, Roger Rookie was walking around AMS when Karl Chameleon waved him in. Roger was pleased with the significant changes in Karl's teaching and overall attitude and was, in fact, amazed how much a teacher could transform himself in one year with the right attitude and support.

After small talk about the upcoming Thanksgiving break, Karl told Roger, "There is something I want to discuss with you, boss, but I'm a little hesitant."

Roger asked, "What's holding you back?"

"Well, you have been great to work with this year, but I am still reminded of how radically different your leadership styles were last year, and after all, you are my boss."

Roger laughed, and responded, "Fair enough, point taken, Karl. Please share with me what's on your mind. I promise not to go 'Mr. Hyde' on you."

Karl did a quick double take, thinking of last year's teachers' lounge conversation, but kept on point.

"Remember that conversation last year about calculators?"

"Yes, I recall the conversation vividly. I probably told you I would consider it, or we didn't have enough money."

The look on Karl's face told Roger his memory was accurate.

"Do you still need them?"

"Mr. Rookie, our students really do. In fact, some of the math that students are supposed to know for their high-stakes test requires they know how to use those special functions that only the graphing calculators provide. Our current calculators are simply unequipped. They're not helping the learning."

"No kidding."

"Yep, Mr. Rookie. What used to be a *want* is now truly a *need*."

Roger assured Karl, "I'll find a way to get you a classroom set of calculators, and if I am unsuccessful, it will be my fault. Learning centeredness starts with the principal."

Karl thanked Roger for listening and supporting him. After a high-five, Roger continued visiting teachers in their classrooms, striving for a balance of climate and accountability as he moved through the year as an instructional leader.

Concluding Year Two

Kris Bliss greeted the superintendent when he walked into the front office at Anywhere Middle School. It had been seven months since the Board of Education had acted on Trudy Savage's resignation, and since then, Kris had moved to the main secretary chair. The district had hired Joy Daily as the other secretary.

Trudy Savage's resignation piqued Mr. Superintendent's interest, and he wanted to see for himself what Roger Rookie was up to. Something was actually "done" about a problem, and he liked that.

I'll take a Rookie over a Neverthere any day, he mused.

Roger Rookie walked into his office and saw Mr. Superintendent reading the assortment of thank-you letters Roger had received from students and parents. "Good morning, sir. What can I do for you today?"

Mr. Superintendent turned and shook Roger's hand. "Rookie, how are things going over here? Be straight with me. Give me the facts. Do we have a focus on learning, or is it just smoke and mirrors and a little bit of Rookie luck on your part?"

Roger smiled and said, "Things are going really well. I'm not going to lie; we have a lot more work to do, but the leadership team has established some ambitious goals, and I could not be prouder of the faculty and staff for the effort they give every day to help our students. Our conversations revolve around learning."

"What about leadership, Rookie? So, yeah, you can move out a secretary with an anger management problem, but can you lead *people*? Can you get the Joe Averages and Martha Middle-of-the-Roads to perform and raise those test scores?"

"Well, for starters, sir, I think I have discovered the secret *and* the path to a school-wide focus on learning. I have found that every time I ratchet-up accountability, I need to do the same with climate. They work in tandem. By addressing both, enhanced learning becomes the focus of conversation. It's a shift that takes time, but we're moving ahead. Here, let me show you." Roger pulled out his notebook and turned to his most recent sketch.

THE GLAD-HANDER
THE PATH TO SUCCESS
THE PATHFINDER
THE HIBERNATOR
THE THUMB
CLIMATE
ACCOUNTABILITY
ME
CAVE
(Hibernating)
PRINCIPAL

"Don't show me a grad school conceptual model, Rookie; just tell me how you're doing it! You say you've got the secret? Give me an example of how it works in plain English!"

"First of all, sir, Kris Bliss taking over in the front office has been one of the three biggest reasons the climate of the school is changing so quickly and dramatically. Joy Daily is a big help too. Because of the hundreds of telephone conversations and front-desk visits they handle each week, parents really feel our school is on their side. Because our parents feel supported, they then support us when we ratchet-up accountability, whether it's responding to a request for them to come to parent-teacher conferences or to check on homework in book bags each night."

Roger continued. "When faculty or staff come to the office, Kris and Joy do what they can immediately to help their professional lives become better, and this frees them up to concentrate on what they do best—educating kids and holding themselves accountable for the learning that takes place."

"Yeah, yeah, yeah, I can see where everybody holding hands and singing 'We are the World' has its benefits. So tell me what else is working. Get to the meat and potatoes, Rookie!"

"Okay, sir, the Bullies no longer run the school."

"Wait, Rookie. I haven't heard that term in years. I think I started teaching with some of them! Are Morose and Slacker still around, sucking air and squandering my tax dollars? Didn't I fix that with an early retirement incentive a few years back?"

Roger almost laughed out loud. "No, sir, they're still here; however, I placed Mildred Morose on a professional improvement plan and am hopeful that, with support, she will make the necessary changes and begin thinking about students' needs and not just her personal wants. Judy Slacker has yet to get on board, but she is no longer causing trouble. There are probably a few from that group whom you don't know, but I'm happy to say last year's bullies-in-training, Edgar Sleeper and LaVon Babble, have already left that group. Although they still require a lot of attention and support, they are joining the AMS team and have embraced the changes we have implemented."

"Just don't be afraid to send me another name for a board meeting, Rookie, if you need to hike up your britches and get rid of someone else!"

"I'll not hesitate, sir."

"Rookie, let me tell you something. After seeing what's been going on around here, I'm here to tell you the biggest reason this school is headed in the right direction is because the students and staff are finally getting the leadership they deserve. And, no, I'm not talking about you! Well, ok, you're part of it. But *all* of your team is showing impressive leadership at *all* levels. It's trickling down to students. Because you've worked to get the jerks and bullies out of the way, your most effective teachers are taking active roles as leaders."

"Thank you, sir, for noticing."

"It's the beginning of a new day at Anywhere, Rookie. You have instilled a focus on learning I hope continues long after I'm greeting folks at the shopping center down the street."

After seeing Mr. Superintendent out of the office, Roger thought about the shift in paradigm that a focus on both climate and accountability had created. He was very glad indeed to see how that shift was moving learning in the right direction. He reflected on how far things at AMS had come.

Sure, we still have passionate discussions at meetings, except now we are no longer wasting time debating who should cover lunch duty; instead, we spend our limited professional development time in collaborative teams reviewing data, discussing instruction, and helping our students ensure better learning, he thought. *When a student or staff member does something worthy of celebration, we celebrate. We have dedicated and caring teachers serving as mentors, teaching and modeling to our beginning teachers that we are in education to help students. We are collectively focused on learning at Anywhere Middle School.*

Mindful of such, Roger's leadership team hosted Anywhere Middle School's first all-school academic assembly at the end of the school year to congratulate students and staff for the improvements made on the curriculum-based assessments as well as their classroom grades. Everyone anticipated receiving higher standardized achievement test scores this year. The leadership team also commended faculty on the co-teaching model that had been a huge success. No one had suspected it would benefit all AMS students so quickly and dramatically.

Data on achievement was now climbing. At the current pace of improvement, in another few years, scores would be through the roof. Great things were taking on a life of their own as the leadership team and entire faculty focused on ways to improve teaching and learning.

Looking out over the assembly, Roger smiled and thought, *If we fall short of the lofty goals we set, it won't be for lack of effort. With attention on both climate and accountability, our learning centeredness has created a refreshing shift from focusing on the wants of adults to focusing on the needs of students. As long as we continue doing that, good things will continue to happen.*

Teachers' Lounge

"What in the heck are you doing with that 'connect-the-dots' contraption, Mildred," said Judy Slacker. "You're beginning to worry me!"

"It's a pacing guide for my curriculum, Slacker. You should know that. Better take a good look. One of these darned things is going to be in your future as well. You're on Rookie's rotation for next fall's evaluations, and he'll put you on the clock."

"Sure, just let him try. I operate on one time clock: Slacker Standard Time."

"Yeah, yeah, yeah," Mildred said, turning her attention back to the pacing guide.

"Hey, where's everybody today?" Slacker wondered.

The Coffee Klatch

"Hey, you guys hear the one about how many principals it takes to win the pie-eating contest at the pep assembly?" Karl Chameleon asked.

"Better be careful, Karl," Nellie said with a smile. "With all those calculators Mr. Rookie just bought for you, you'd be ill-timed to make wise cracks about beating him in the pep assembly's tricycle race—or the kids shaving his head after those gains in our reading levels."

"Yeah, he was a pretty good sport, wasn't he?" said Karl. "I'm actually going to miss the boss a bit this summer. We're heading to the Florida Keys this year. Can't wait!"

"Just make sure you schedule your family trip around our leadership team retreat, if you can," Sandy Starr said. "Mr. Rookie is pulling out all the stops with some team building. Rumor has it whitewater rafting is involved."

"That will be great!" Nellie Newcomer said.

"Hey, everybody!" Edgar Sleeper said, entering the room.

"Edgarrrrrrrr!" everyone shouted in unison.

Edgar loved coming to a place where everybody knew his name. Someone quickly set a cup of his favorite coffee, made his way, in front of him. He took a sip and said, "I can't stay long, guys. Got my evaluation appointment with Mr. Rookie today, and I think he'll be quite happy with my work on assessments. I just wanted to wish you all a great summer if I don't see you all before the end of the week."

Edgar downed the coffee quickly and left.

"I'm really glad he came," said Nellie.

"Great guy," Karl said. "You hear the way kids are talking about his class lately?"

Sandy Starr smiled. *It feels good to be around such positive people,* she thought to herself. Nellie Newcomer had been a bit part in Sandy Starr's own transformation this past year, as she found she was getting as much out of the mentor/protégé relationship as was Nellie.

The chemistry in the Coffee Klatch was just right and had proven to be a catalyst to building-wide camaraderie.

Sandy thought to herself, as she poured her last cup of coffee for the year, *Nellie sure is growing in her own leadership, and it seems to be rubbing off on the faculty.* She had seen a clear improvement in terms of motivation and energy for creative classroom teaching and learning. *In fact, our colleagues are behaving more like Nellie and adopting her student-centered approach to learning. Maybe the days of our teachers being more focused on their own wants rather than the needs of the students are behind us.*

Chapter 6
Back to the Big Night...
"That's a Wrap"

"That's simply an incredible story, Roger," Carol Charming said. "I can really see why you're being given the Super Apple award by the State Principals Association. You changed and grew yourself as a leader, and it appears that by figuring out the secret path toward a learning-centered school, you have helped everyone at Anywhere Middle School change for the good of your entire community."

"Well, thank you, Carol. But, again, I'm just so very lucky my faculty and staff gave me a chance. I made plenty of mistakes, but when I failed, they allowed me to 'fail forward' and discover the secret to better learning and leadership. I've received a lot of wonderful advice and guidance along the way. Plus I get to meet great folks like yourself, Carol! That's certainly a bonus."

"Mr. Rookie, two minutes before your introduction on stage," said Kris Bliss, who was at his side and coordinating everything this evening— seamlessly, pleasantly, and responsibly.

"Carol, you'll love hearing Mr. Rookie when he speaks," Kris said. "He is very inspirational."

"Ms. Bliss needs to do more under-promising, so I can have a chance of over-delivering," Roger said to Carol with a chuckle.

"Thanks for your time, Roger," Carol said as she stood. "I'd better let you go and get back to my place in the reporters' pool, but aside from this story, can I ask you a question?"

"Sure, Carol."

"Would you mind if we got together next week for a quick snack or soda, just to hang out? I work a lot of hours like you, so my schedule is pretty tight, but they have a new place in town called 'The Popcorn Wagon' just down the street. One hundred different flavors; my favorite is Kettle Corn #3. It's just that I'm so glad to meet you and would like to get to know you better, if you don't mind."

Wow! Roger thought. *The Popcorn Wagon! I've been so busy lately, I haven't had much time to think about stuff like hanging out, let alone with a cute young reporter who thinks I'm an okay guy.*

"I'd love to, Carol! It would be awesome."

Carol Charming strolled to the press area. When he walked to the podium, she offered Roger a warm smile and a wave.

THE PATHFINDER EFFECTS ON STAFF...

SUPERSTARS

- Feel empowered
- Have unlimited energy
- Willingly take chances and collaborate

FENCESITTERS

- Move toward the superstars
- Want to associate with a winner
- Try harder than they thought possible...collaborate...and LIKE IT!

BULLIES

- Have dramatically reduced power and influence
- Change or leave
- Become very isolated

THE PATHFINDER CONTINUED...

THE LEADER FEELS

- Great Satisfaction
- Ready to take on the NEXT CHALLENGE
- PROUD!

UNINTENDED CONSEQUENCES

- Everybody wants to work at YOUR SCHOOL
- Instead of the leader being the only source of morale, it now comes from everywhere
- FAME, FORTUNE, AND YOU GET THE GIRL!!! :)

The Epilogue

Thanks for reading. We hope you enjoyed our story.

The parable of *The Secret Solution* brings to life many of the personalities and moods we educators see in our own settings every day. It's very likely you have experience with one (or perhaps all) of the four leadership personalities Roger went through in this book. And we're willing to bet you recognized a few friends and colleagues. Although Sandy Starr, Judy Slacker, and the other characters in the books are obviously caricaturized to the extreme, they resonate with us because their traits are so close to the truth. When we watch television shows like *The Office* or *Saturday Night Live*, the more closely the characters depict their real-life counterparts, the more significance they have for us. By presenting the characters in this fashion, it is also easier to see what happens to them as the leader alters the approach taken in leadership and management.

We intentionally included some deeper issues related to school culture in our story. We've heard from many leaders who have shared parts of this parable to discuss touchy topics with their faculty and staff members, as the stories provide the "cover" necessary to talk about people close by as if they are not close by at all. We hope this book gives you the ability to leverage similar conversations to help improve your own school culture.

We have learned, through experience and observation, that most people can verbally describe an effective leader; however, actually *doing leadership* on a regular basis is a much more significant challenge. As Roger Rookie learned, it takes a commitment to finding the best ways to communicate with and encourage your staff, and, very often, that means looking within oneself and starting over when things aren't going the way we want them to.

Another idea we wanted to represent in the book is the informal, yet powerful, influence others have in an organization. In many settings, peers can be intimidating, not only to their colleagues but also to their principal.

Bullying, for example, happens downward, but bullies also inflict their actions upon peers laterally and even those above them on the organizational chart. Leaders must have an awareness of what effect a bully's actions have on a school, just as they seek to understand how their own leadership behavior affects informal dynamics.

In this final section, we'll recap the different leadership styles displayed in *The Secret Solution*. We encourage you to take some time to reflect on your own desired leadership style. If you are a future leader, this exercise may help you identify what type of a leader you would like to be. If you are a current leader, you may find areas where you can improve. As you think about or discuss different styles, habits, and practices of leaders, you may discover new ways to encourage or mentor your teachers and ways to help other leaders grow.

The Hibernator

In our work as school leaders and trainers, we have seen people like Roger who struggle with focusing on the busywork, feeling productive in the paperwork and, at the same time, demonstrating ineptitude in their leadership of people. They mistakenly think being a highly organized person is a key characteristic for a quality school leader and spend too much time in an office taking care of procedural tasks.

Hibernators' avoidance of conflict opens the door for those with controlling and negative personalities to drive school culture. Very often, their neglect to address issues comes back to bite them in the form of gossip, passive aggression, and outright negative behaviors.

It is no fun dealing with domineering, negative people, but it is essential that a leader does so. Retreating to the safety of one's office may allow us to temporarily avoid dealing with uncomfortable people and issues, but the issues we're hiding from will not magically go away; in fact, left unaddressed, those issues often grow. Negativity is like a virus or bacteria: Left untreated, it's going to spread. Some staff members may use the absence of leadership as an opportunity to influence others in a negative way. Also, when a leader stays in avoidance mode, the people who want to do the right thing are much more vulnerable, as they feel isolated and alone, which ironically is exactly how the leader feels.

Hibernators Often:

- Stay in their offices
- Avoid having staff meetings
- Do not take the time to get to know students and staff
- Leave the building whenever possible
- Avoid others who have strong personalities
- Can be seen as invisible or ghost-like
- May have a great deal of internal anxiety

Questions for Personal Reflection (or Group Discussion)

- What were some of the challenges Roger experienced in Chapter 2 to which you could relate personally?
- Do you have, or have you had, any Hibernators in your school/district?
- How does this heads-down approach to leadership impact . . .
  - o Teacher involvement/camaraderie?
  - o School climate?
  - o School culture?
  - o Student success?
  - o The leader's own personal and professional satisfaction?
- What proactive actions can a leader take to avoid behaving like a Hibernator?

Hibernators, like most school leaders, want to be good leaders. They care about education, their students, and their staffs, but they feel uncomfortable or ill-equipped to deal with conflict or to say no, even to unreasonable requests.

If we find ourselves in hibernation mode, it is essential we require ourselves to interact with others. We must press through the apprehension, even if doing so feels painful. Our mere presence can help the people we supervise feel safer and more secure. Getting "out there" also empowers us to see that the feeling of fear is often worse than whatever is causing the worry. Spending time with other leaders who seem more comfortable dealing with tough situations is one way to learn how to initiate or engage in conversations and communicate informally. And if you ask them how they manage to handle conflict and confrontations so well, you'll probably discover they have their own apprehensions as well; they've just learned to press through them. A Hibernator must follow the idea of the classic book, *Feel the Fear . . . and Do It Anyway.*

Every time you step out of your office and stand up as a leader, you'll get better at it. All of us, at times, want to avoid conflict and pressure. That's natural. But it is imperative not to be a Hibernator. Habitual avoidance will limit, or even eliminate, your effectiveness as a leader.

The Glad-hander

When a person transitions into leadership, it is not uncommon to rely heavily on relationships while trying to please people. Glad-handers excel in the critical, relational area of leadership; however, they can bring with them the inability or unwillingness to confront issues or problems.

Unlike a Hibernator, where a lack of visibility and an avoidance of conflict result in a negative school climate, a Glad-hander's focus on developing relationships and pleasing people actually results in a positive climate. Unfortunately, those good feelings come at the expense of a healthy school culture. The areas where conflict aversion creates problems for Glad-handers include leading school improvement initiatives, delivering authentic staff evaluations, and making unpopular decisions. All of these actions require a leader's ability to facilitate change efforts where there will most likely be opposition—and a Glad-hander avoids being in that position. Because discomfort always accompanies any change, the Glad-hander does not move a school toward positive change.

The Epilogue

A major problem with Glad-hander leadership is the fact that staff members will eventually realize the leader will not confront them at any time. They will also realize the leader will not confront others, no matter how toxic the environment has become. When bullies know they can run the school, decisions become self-centered, and students' learning suffers as a result.

Glad-handers Often:
- Will not give a definitive answer when presented with a difficult situation
- Delay actions or never implement them due to paralysis-by-avoidance
- Provide overly positive feedback even when not appropriate, including evaluations, which impinges upon a leader's credibility
- Reward disproportionately those who have strong personalities
- Demonstrate an inability in leading change successfully
- Fail to guarantee or improve teaching and learning
- Experience a great deal of internal anxiety

Questions for Personal Reflection (or Group Discussion)
- What were some of the challenges Roger experienced in Chapter 3 to which you could relate personally?
- Do you have, or have you had, any Glad-handers in your school/district?
- How does the "everybody's friend" approach to leadership impact . . .
    - o Teacher involvement/camaraderie?
    - o School climate?
    - o School culture?
    - o Student success?
    - o The leader's own personal and professional satisfaction?
- What proactive actions can a leader take to avoid becoming a Glad-hander?

College preparatory programs train prospective teachers in student behavior-management skills and techniques. Most educators are experienced at confronting students and skilled at eliminating negative behaviors and reinforcing positive behaviors. Glad-handers are unable to transfer their effective behavior-management skills when dealing with adults.

Confronting adults is like any other skill in that it takes practice, coaching, and reflection to improve. If you are a leader, there is nothing wrong with delaying a confrontational conversation; however, avoiding the confrontational conversation will eventually cause major problems for yourself and others.

The Thumb

A Thumb style of leadership is very different from the Hibernator and Glad-hander. Whereas those styles of leadership avoid confrontation, the Thumb invites confrontation, to a fault.

A catastrophic problem of this style of leadership is that the lack of relationships combined with a very direct (possibly attacking) style of communication will eventually result in mutiny, or, in the least, entrenchment. Students, parents, and the community typically will not tolerate a person in a leadership position who consistently behaves in an authoritarian style. Look no further than college or professional sports; teams filled with coaches who dominate with an iron fist are now more the exception than the rule. Those types of coaches are almost extinct because their lack of positive, trusting relationships eventually leads to termination.

Thumbs Often:
- Do not establish, develop, or nurture positive relationships
- Refuse to seek out or listen to faculty and staff input
- Punish those who question or fail to follow their demands
- Influence the good people to leave the organization
- Cause a great deal of anxiety in their faculty and staff, which can trickle down to students

The Epilogue

Questions for Personal Reflection (or Group Discussion)

- What were some of the challenges Roger experienced in Chapter 4 to which you could relate personally?
- Do you have, or have you had, any Thumbs in your school/district?
- How does the "my way or the highway" approach to leadership impact . . .
  - o Teacher involvement/camaraderie?
  - o School climate?
  - o School culture?
  - o Student success?
  - o The leader's own personal and professional satisfaction?
- What proactive actions can a leader take to avoid becoming a Thumb?

An important trait for quality leaders is that they surround themselves with people who are comfortable disagreeing with them or telling them no. Robert Kelley, in his work, *In Praise of Followers*, talks of challenges in followership in terms how people behave like sheep, yes-people, or as alienated followers, when not effective. Those who behave like sheep are overly passive and uncritical of anything leadership brings to the table. They just take up space and do not advance the mission of an organization. Yes-people are more active in promoting mission, yet are uncritical of anything leadership says or does, and thus do not serve as a leader's watchful eye. Those who are alienated followers are passive and do not do much to advance mission, but they fill that gap in productivity by being critical in front of audiences who will listen, and thus, through their toxic messaging, work against what leadership is trying to do. Thumbs can bring about these characteristics in people. What Thumbs cannot do is provide for an environment where effective followers are positive and actively engaged in work furthering the mission yet able to challenge their leaders to make the best decisions. Effective followers are not empowered on a Thumb's watch. They are driven out.

Even the best of leaders can let emotion or past experiences cloud a decision. Without confidants to tell us what we *need* to hear versus what we want (or demand) to hear, we may make poor decisions. Refusing to embrace this trait of listening, Thumbs may run headlong into disaster and take down their schools with them.

In our experiences as educators, consultants, and administrators, we have noticed that, although the Thumb style of leadership still exists, it is less common than the other types. It is very difficult to survive in an educational profession as an authoritarian except possibly during rare emergencies requiring quick decisions to put out fires, with no time for consensus.

The Pathfinder

Unlike the Hibernator, Glad-hander, and Thumb—where deficits seem to offset any positives in leadership—a Pathfinder finds the balance between leading climate positively and leveraging accountability. This leader moves the school toward a successful and healthy school culture. Students and staff feel safe and like being a part of a Pathfinder's school, and, equally as important, they experience success.

Pathfinders cultivate school cultures that are infectious in their efficacy, and people want to be a part of them. Former students and retired staff members look back on this school with fond memories experienced, thankful for the opportunities provided to them as professionals and lifelong learners. They know their children and grandchildren are in good hands because Pathfinders are equipping them with what they need in life, and, through modeling, what they will need throughout their lives in leadership. Pathfinder principals provide more than leadership and management; they teach *a way of living*.

When Pathfinders lead, students and staff help reinforce established expectations regarding behavior, productivity, and the definition of what it means to be successful. They are authentic in how they relate to one another and act as if they have two ears and one mouth for a reason. Why?

134

The Epilogue

Because they see leaders at all levels doing that—in the principal's office, in the classrooms, in the cafeteria, and in the hallways. The balance of high positive climate and authentic accountability provides a path on which all can travel to success. It's a path that works at every level of schooling and for persons of any age.

When Pathfinders leave their schools for new leadership opportunities, the school cultures and initiatives do not suffer because the leader has distributed leadership, responsibility, and motivation to succeed throughout the school. Faculty and staff members know how to lead and how to follow, and they will continue to do the good work.

Pathfinders improve faculty and staff performance through clarity of feedback, effective coaching, fair allocation of resources, and prioritizing their time and energy to make improvements through shared decision-making. Pathfinders always work with children's futures in mind, which sometimes requires counseling adults out of jobs and even firing people. Staff members unable or unwilling to make the necessary changes a Pathfinder requests and requires will professionally and respectfully facilitate their own departures. Pathfinders recognize the talents people do have and will talent-scout appropriately, and when all the key positions are staffed as best they can be, Pathfinders maintain a positive energy and the personal accountability to do what they must to leverage team success.

Pathfinders Often:
- Create a shared vision with faculty and staff
- Ensure learning is at the center of decision-making
- Maintain a high visibility of leadership in classrooms, in the hallways—anywhere students and staff congregate
- Recognize students and staff frequently, appropriately, and in ways that are individualized for their needs
- Demonstrate proactivity in developing expectations so people who do not meet expectations are handled quickly, respectfully, and responsibly

- Ensure relationships, relationships, and relationships marry nicely with accountability, accountability, and accountability
- Communicate with internal and external stakeholders in an ongoing and authentic manner

Questions for Personal Reflection (or Group Discussion)

- What were some of the challenges Roger experienced in Chapter 5 to which you could relate personally?
- Do you have, or have you had, any Pathfinders in your school/ district?
- How does a Pathfinder's approach to leadership impact . . .
  - o Teacher/staff involvement/camaraderie?
  - o School culture?
  - o School climate?
  - o Student success?
  - o The leader's own personal and professional satisfaction?
- What actions can a leader take to become a Pathfinder?

School leadership is an incredibly difficult job. We, the authors of this book, have lived the mistakes in Roger's journey. We call them *opportunities for wisdom*; however, in our observations, school leadership preparation, professional development, and professional learning opportunities are helping more leaders in their journeys to becoming Pathfinders than ever before in our profession.

Like Roger—like us—*you*, too, can become a Pathfinder!

More from

DAVE BURGESS Consulting, Inc.

Teach Like a PIRATE
Increase Student Engagement, Boost Your Creativity, and Transform Your Life as an Educator
By Dave Burgess (@BurgessDave)

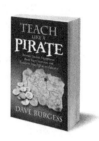

New York Times' bestseller *Teach Like a PIRATE* sparked a worldwide educational revolution with its passionate teaching manifesto and dynamic student-engagement strategies. Translated into multiple languages, it sparks outrageously creative lessons and life-changing student experiences.

P is for PIRATE
Inspirational ABCs for Educators
By Dave and Shelley Burgess (@Burgess_Shelley)

In *P is for Pirate*, husband-and-wife team Dave and Shelley Burgess tap personal experiences of seventy educators to inspire others to create fun and exciting places to learn. It's a wealth of imaginative and creative ideas that makes learning and teaching more fulfilling than ever before.

The Innovator's Mindset
Empower Learning, Unleash Talent, and Lead a Culture of Creativity
By George Couros (@gcouros)

In *The Innovator's Mindset*, teachers and administrators discover that compliance to a scheduled curriculum hinders student innovation, critical thinking, and creativity. To become forward-thinking leaders, students must be empowered to wonder and explore.

Pure Genius
Building a Culture of Innovation and Taking 20% Time to the Next Level
By Don Wettrick (@DonWettrick)

Collaboration—with experts, students, and other educators—helps create interesting and even life-changing opportunities for learning. In *Pure Genius*, Don Wettrick inspires and equips educators with a systematic blueprint for beating classroom boredom and teaching innovation.

Learn Like a PIRATE
Empower Your Students to Collaborate, Lead, and Succeed
By Paul Solarz (@PaulSolarz)

Passing grades don't equip students for life and career responsibilities. *Learn Like a PIRATE* shows how risk-taking and exploring passions in stimulating, motivating, supportive, self-directed classrooms creates students capable of making smart, responsible decisions on their own.

Ditch That Textbook
Free Your Teaching and Revolutionize Your Classroom
By Matt Miller (@jmattmiller)

Ditch That Textbook creates a support system, toolbox, and manifesto that can free teachers from outdated textbooks. Miller empowers them to untether themselves, throw out meaningless, pedestrian teaching and learning practices, and evolve and revolutionize their classrooms.

50 Things You Can Do with Google Classroom
By Alice Keeler and Libbi Miller (@alicekeeler, @MillerLibbi)

50 Things You Can Do with Google Classroom provides a thorough overview of this GAfE app and shortens the teacher learning curve for introducing technology in the classroom. Keeler and Miller's ideas, instruction, and screenshots help teachers go digital with this powerful tool.

50 Things to Go Further with Google Classroom
A Student-Centered Approach
By Alice Keeler and Libbi Miller (@alicekeeler, @MillerLibbi)

In *50 Things to Go Further with Google Classroom: A Student-Centered Approach*, authors and educators Alice Keeler and Libbi Miller help teachers create a digitally rich, engaging, student-centered environment that taps the power of individualized learning using Google Classroom.

140 Twitter Tips for Educators
Get Connected, Grow Your Professional Learning Network, and Reinvigorate Your Career
By Brad Currie, Billy Krakower, and Scott Rocco (@bradmcurrie, @wkrakower, @ScottRRocco)

In *140 Twitter Tips for Educators*, #Satchat hosts and founders of Evolving Educators, Brad Currie, Billy Krakower, and Scott Rocco, offer step-by-step instruction on Twitter basics and building an online following within Twitter's vibrant network of educational professionals.

Master the Media
How Teaching Media Literacy Can Save Our Plugged-In World
By Julie Smith (@julnilsmith)

Master the Media explains media history, purpose, and messaging so teachers and parents can empower students with critical-thinking skills which lead to informed choices, the ability to differentiate between truth and lies, and discern perception from reality. Media literacy can save the world.

The Zen Teacher
Creating Focus, Simplicity, and Tranquility in the Classroom
By Dan Tricarico (@thezenteacher)

Unrushed and fully focused, teachers influence—even improve—the future when they maximize performance and improve their quality of life. In *The Zen Teacher*, Dan Tricarico offers practical, easy-to-use techniques to develop a non-religious Zen practice and thrive in the classroom.

eXPlore Like a Pirate
Gamification and Game-Inspired Course Design to Engage, Enrich, and Elevate Your Learners
By Michael Matera (@MrMatera)

Create an experiential, collaborative, and creative world with classroom game designer and educator Michael Matera's game-based learning book, *eXPlore Like a Pirate*. Matera helps teachers apply motivational gameplay techniques and enhance curriculum with gamification strategies.

Your School Rocks . . . So Tell People!
Passionately Pitch and Promote the Positives Happening on Your Campus
By Ryan McLane and Eric Lowe (@McLane_Ryan, @EricLowe21)

Your School Rocks . . . So Tell People! helps schools create effective social media communication strategies that keep students' families and the community connected to what's going on at school, offering more than seventy immediately actionable tips with easy-to-follow instructions and video tutorial links.

Play Like a Pirate
Engage Students with Toys, Games, and Comics
By Quinn Rollins (@jedikermit)

In *Play Like a Pirate*, Quinn Rollins offers practical, engaging strategies and resources that make it easy to integrate fun into your curriculum. Regardless of grade level, serious learning can be seriously fun with inspirational ideas that engage students in unforgettable ways.

The Classroom Chef
Sharpen Your Lessons. Season Your Classes. Make Math Meaningful
By John Stevens and Matt Vaudrey (@Jstevens009, @MrVaudrey)

With imagination and preparation, every teacher can be *The Classroom Chef* using John Stevens and Matt Vaudrey's secret recipes, ingredients, and tips that help students "get" math. Use ideas as-is, or tweak to create enticing educational meals that engage students.

How Much Water Do We Have?
5 Success Principles for Conquering Any Challenge and Thriving in Times of Change
By Pete Nunweiler with Kris Nunweiler

Stressed out, overwhelmed, or uncertain at work or home? It could be figurative dehydration. *How Much Water Do We Have?* identifies five key elements necessary for success of any goal, life transition, or challenge. Learn to find, acquire, and use the 5 Waters of Success.

The Writing on the Classroom Wall
How Posting Your Most Passionate Beliefs about Education Can Empower Your Students, Propel Your Growth, and Lead to a Lifetime of Learning
By Steve Wyborney (@SteveWyborney)

Big ideas lead to deeper learning, but they don't have to be profound to have profound impact. Teacher Steve Wyborney explains why and how sharing ideas sharpens and refines them. It's okay if some ideas fall off the wall; what matters most is sharing and discussing.

Kids Deserve It!
Pushing Boundaries and Challenging Conventional Thinking
By Todd Nesloney and Adam Welcome (@TechNinjaTodd, @awelcome)

Think big. Make learning fun and meaningful. *Kids Deserve It!* Nesloney and Welcome offer high-tech, high-touch, and highly engaging practices that inspire risk-taking and shake up the status quo on behalf of your students. Rediscover why you became an educator, too!

LAUNCH
Using Design Thinking to Boost Creativity and Bring Out the Maker in Every Student
By John Spencer and A.J. Juliani (@spencerideas, @ajjuliani)

When students identify themselves as makers, inventors, and creators, they discover powerful problem-solving and critical-thinking skills. Their imaginations and creativity will shape our future. John Spencer and A.J. Juliani's *LAUNCH* process dares you to innovate and empower them.

Instant Relevance
Using Today's Experiences to Teach Tomorrow's Lessons
By Denis Sheeran (@MathDenisNJ)

Learning sticks when it's relevant to students. In *Instant Relevance*, author and keynote speaker Denis Sheeran equips you to create engaging lessons *from* experiences and events that matter to students while helping them make meaningful connections between the real world and the classroom.

Escaping the School Leader's Dunk Tank
How to Prevail When Others Want to See You Drown
By Rebecca Coda and Rick Jetter (@RebeccaCoda, @RickJetter)

Dunk-tank situations—discrimination, bad politics, revenge, or ego-driven coworkers—can make an educator's life miserable. Coda and Jetter (dunk-tank survivors themselves) share real-life stories and insightful research to equip school leaders with tools to survive and, better yet, avoid getting "dunked."

Start. Right. Now.
Teach and Lead for Excellence
By Todd Whitaker, Jeff Zoul, and Jimmy Casas (@ToddWhitaker, @Jeff_Zoul, @casas_jimmy)

Excellent leaders and teachers *Know the Way, Show the Way, Go the Way, and Grow Each Day*. Whitaker, Zoul, and Casas share four key behaviors of excellence from educators across the U.S. and motivate to put you on the right path.

Lead Like a PIRATE
Make School Amazing for Your Students and Staff
By Shelley Burgess and Beth Houf (@Burgess_Shelley, @BethHouf)

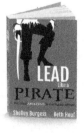

Lead Like a PIRATE maps out character traits necessary to captain a school or district. You'll learn where to find treasure already in your classrooms and schools—and bring out the best in educators. Find encouragement in your relentless quest to make school amazing for everyone!

Teaching Math with Google Apps
50 G Suite Activities
By Alice Keeler and Diana Herrington (@AliceKeeler, @mathdiana)

Teaching Math with Google Apps meshes the easy student/teacher interaction of Google Apps with G Suite that empowers student creativity and critical thinking. Keeler and Herrington demonstrate fifty ways to bring math classes into the twenty-first century with easy-to-use technology.

Table Talk Math
A Practical Guide for Bringing Math into Everyday Conversations
By John Stevens (@Jstevens009)

In *Table Talk Math*, John Stevens offers parents—and teachers—ideas for initiating authentic, math-based, everyday conversations that get kids to notice and pique their curiosity about the numbers, patterns, and equations in the world around them.

Shift This!
How to Implement Gradual Change for Massive Impact in Your Classroom
By Joy Kirr (@JoyKirr)

Establishing a student-led culture focused on individual responsibility and personalized learning *is* possible, sustainable, and even easy when it happens little by little. In *Shift This!*, Joy Kirr details gradual shifts in thinking, teaching, and approach for massive impact in your classroom.

Unmapped Potential
An Educator's Guide to Lasting Change
By Julie Hasson and Missy Lennard (@PPrincipals)

Overwhelmed and overworked? You're not alone, but it can get better. You simply need the right map to guide you from frustrated to fulfilled. *Unmapped Potential* offers advice and practical strategies to forge a unique path to becoming the educator and *person* you want to be.

Shattering the Perfect Teacher Myth
6 Truths That Will Help You THRIVE as an Educator
By Aaron Hogan (@aaron_hogan)

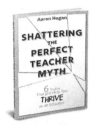

Author and educator Aaron Hogan helps shatter the idyllic "perfect teacher" myth, which erodes self-confidence with unrealistic expectations and sets teachers up for failure. His book equips educators with strategies that help them shift out of survival mode and THRIVE.

Social LEADia
Moving Students from Digital Citizenship to Digital Leadership
By Jennifer Casa-Todd (@JCasaTodd)

A networked society requires students to leverage social media to connect to people, passions, and opportunities to grow and make a difference. *Social LEADia* helps shift focus at school and home from digital citizenship to digital leadership and equip students for the future.

Spark Learning
3 Keys to Embracing the Power of Student Curiosity
By Ramsey Musallam (@ramusallam)

Inspired by his popular TED Talk "3 Rules to *Spark Learning*," Musallam combines brain science research, proven teaching methods, and his personal story to empower you to improve your students' learning experiences by inspiring inquiry and harnessing its benefits.

Ditch That Homework
Practical Strategies to Help Make Homework Obsolete
By Matt Miller and Alice Keeler (@jmattmiller, @alicekeeler)

In *Ditch That Homework*, Miller and Keeler discuss the pros and cons of homework, why it's assigned, and what life could look like without it. They evaluate research, share parent and teacher insights, then make a convincing case for ditching it for effective and personalized learning methods.

The Four O'Clock Faculty
A Rogue Guide to Revolutionizing Professional
Development
By Rich Czyz (@RACzyz)

In *The Four O'Clock Faculty*, Rich identifies ways to make professional learning meaningful, efficient, and, above all, personally relevant. It's a practical guide to revolutionize PD, revealing why some is so awful and what you can do to change the model for the betterment of everyone.

Culturize
Every Student. Every Day. Whatever It Takes.
By Jimmy Casas (@casas_jimmy)

Culturize dives into what it takes to cultivate a community of learners who embody innately human traits our world desperately needs—kindness, honesty, and compassion. Casas's stories reveal how "soft skills" can be honed while exceeding academic standards of twenty-first-century learning.

Code Breaker
Increase Creativity, Remix Assessment, and Develop a
Class of Coder Ninjas!
By Brian Aspinall (@mraspinall)

You don't have to be a "computer geek" to use coding to turn curriculum expectations into student skills. Use *Code Breaker* to teach students how to identify problems, develop solutions, and use computational thinking to apply and demonstrate learning.

The Wild Card
7 Steps to an Educator's Creative Breakthrough
By Hope and Wade King (@hopekingteach, @wadeking7)

The Kings facilitate a creative breakthrough in the classroom with *The Wild Card*, a step-by-step guide to drawing on your authentic self to deliver your content creatively and be the *wild card* who changes the game for your learners.

Stories from Webb
The Ideas, Passions, and Convictions of a Principal and His School Family
By Todd Nesloney (@TechNinjaTodd)

Stories from Webb goes right to the heart of education. Told by award-winning principal Todd Nesloney and his dedicated team of staff and teachers, this book reminds you why you became an educator. Relatable stories reinvigorate and may inspire you to tell your own!

The Principled Principal
10 Principles for Leading Exceptional Schools
By Jeffrey Zoul and Anthony McConnell (@Jeff_Zou, @mcconnellaw)

Zoul and McConnell know from personal experience that the role of school principal is one of the most challenging *and* the most rewarding in education. Using relatable stories and real-life examples, they reveal ten core values that will empower you to work and lead with excellence.

The Limitless School
Creative Ways to Solve the Culture Puzzle
By Abe Hege and Adam Dovico (@abehege, @adamdovico)

Being intentional about creating a positive culture is imperative for your school's success. This book identifies the nine pillars that support a positive school culture and explains how each stakeholder has a vital role to play in the work of making schools safe, inviting, and dynamic.

Google Apps for Littles
Believe They Can
By Christine Pinto and Alice Keeler (@PintoBeanz11, @alicekeeler)

Learn how to tap into students' natural curiosity using technology. Pinto and Keeler share a wealth of innovative ways to integrate digital tools in the primary classroom to make learning engaging and relevant for even the youngest of today's twenty-first-century learners.

Be the One for Kids
You Have the Power to Change the Life of a Child
By Ryan Sheehy (@sheehyrw)

Students need guidance to succeed academically, but they also need our help to survive and thrive in today's turbulent world. They need someone to model the attributes that will help them win not just in school but in life as well. That someone is *you*.

Let Them Speak
How Student Voice Can Transform Your School
By Rebecca Coda and Rick Jetter (@RebeccaCoda, @RickJetter)

We say, "Student voice matters," but are we really listening? This book will inspire you to find out what your students really think, feel, and need. You'll learn how to listen to and use student feedback to improve your school's culture. All you have to do is ask—and then *Let Them Speak*.

The EduProtocol Field Guide
16 Student-Centered Lesson Frames for Infinite Learning Possibilities
By Marlena Hebren and Jon Corippo (@mhebern, @jcorippo)

Are you ready to break out of the lesson-and-worksheet rut? Use *The EduProtocol Field Guide* to create engaging and effective instruction, build culture, and deliver content to K–12 students in a supportive, creative environment.

All 4s and 5s
A Guide to Teaching and Leading Advanced Placement Programs
Andrew Sharos (@AndrewSharosAP)

AP classes shouldn't be relegated to "privileged" schools and students. With proper support, every student can experience success. *All 4s and 5s* offers a wealth of classroom and program strategies that equip you to develop a culture of academic and personal excellence.

Shake Up Learning
Practical Ideas to Move Learning from Static to Dynamic

By Kasey Bell (@ShakeUpLearning)

Is the learning in your classroom static or dynamic? *Shake Up Learning* guides you through the process of creating dynamic learning opportunities—from purposeful planning and maximizing technology to fearless implementation.

About the Authors

Todd Whitaker is a professor in Educational Leadership at the University of Missouri, Columbia. He is a former teacher and principal as well as emeriti faculty of educational leadership at Indiana State University in Terre Haute.

Sam Miller is the chief administrator at Central Rivers Area Education Agency in Cedar Falls, Iowa. He is a former teacher, principal, and superintendent and serves as a consultant in leadership development and school improvement.

Ryan Donlan is an associate professor in Educational Leadership in the Bayh College of Education of Indiana State University. He is a former teacher, assistant principal, principal, and superintendent. He serves as an authority and trainer in promoting positive human relations, leadership development, and school improvement.

Made in United States
North Haven, CT
07 July 2022

21070470R00089